OPEN WITH YOUR

BROKEN

Remove the Power of Your Past and Gain Freedom in Christ

DANA GOODRUM

FIRST EDITION

ISBN: 978-1-946466-46-4

Library of Congress Control Number: 2018948968

Published by

P.O. Box 2839, Apopka, FL 32704

Acknowledgments

Thanks and praise to God who rescued me from myself, transformed my reflection while repairing His damaged creation.

In honor of my cousin Ryane Jenig. Thank you for recognizing the beautiful broken in everyone. Thank you for loving and celebrating uniqueness, capturing brilliance, and living vibrantly. Thank you for impacting the world with such significance that your ripples turned to waves as they catch the sun bringing genuine light to the shores. Our love for you is immeasurable, and our hearts still ache in your absence.

To my children, Michael and Milan. I am positive there is not yet word to encompass the love, adoration, and pride I have for the both of you. I am humbled daily, that God entrusted me, to be the mother of two incredible human beings. You are amazing, loving, powerful children of God. Thank you for always believing in your mom. I love you more.

To my parents, Joe and Denise. There are a million reasons to thank you; for your sacrifices, advice, patience, and unwavering support. You never once stopped believing that I would change the world. Please know how impactful that has been in my life. Do not ever question how amazing you are or have ever been. I am forever thankful that God chose you for me. I love you both.

To my sister, Erica Denise. Without even knowing, you source in me a drive to keep going. You are the only person on earth who can take away my homesickness by their presence, not my homes. You are my best friend and my biggest supporter. I love making you tear up, big softy. Marley and Kingston, I love you whole bunches.

To my soul sister, Liz. You never let me give up on myself or my dreams, no matter how overwhelmed I was or how many things I was balancing. You are my human. I love you.

To my aunts and uncles. I have been blessed beyond measure to be raised by such amazing, powerful, loving, human beings. You have championed me since the day I was born, and never once stopped. My journey has not been easy, and not always kind, but you prayed, supported, guided, and most importantly, loved. Always trust His divine providence. I love you.

To my cousins, my many cousins. Our family is so rich in love and the legacy our grandparents have left us. We are so blessed. I hope you know how truly thankful I am for each of you and how much I love you. Mountain mover, you are my faith-filled hero.

Theresa & Paul, I love you both so much. Thank you for journeying this faith walk with me in the most amazing ways. You have continued to inspire me, strengthen me, guide me and push me. God appointed you into my life, and I am not sure what I did to deserve such awesome people. I am truly thankful for you, Theresa, and will forever value our friendship. I love you.

To Anndrea, Bobbi, Amber, Keisha, Mia, Shelly, Nikki, Je, Barbara, Jaime, Renee, Audra, Sissy, Davina, Lindsay, Stephanie, Pam, and Sandra. You are my sisters in Christ and have been there for me through this faith walk. I am forever grateful to God for placing you in my life, allowing us to journey this life together, and providing me with such fierce prayer warriors and soldiers to go into battle with.

To my Koke Mill Christian Church Family, Pastor Stan & Rosann Summers, Molly, PJ & Dana, Doug & Brittany, Dave, Suzanne & Bud, Matt, Kerma & Mike, Kelly, Jenny, Sandra & Jim, Pat & Sharon, Sue &

John, John & Shelly, and the many others who have blessed my faith walk. Thank you for allowing me to be open, for being genuine reflections of Jesus, and for truly wanting to grow deeper in your pursuit for Christ. I love each of you so very much.

To Les, Rachel, Zola, and Memphis: We are forever family. Thank you for knowing and loving who I am, even during the times I didn't. Ohana.

To Keely Boeving. Thank you for helping me believe in this project and helping tell my story in a way that made sense to other people as much as it made sense to me. Thank you as a sister in Christ for valuing its transparency and protecting the vulnerability that made this book so unique. You were incredible, professional, and truly inspiring.

Table of Contents

Introduction

If you are reading this book, then I first want to let you know two things: One, I prayed for you long before you decided to purchase this book, before God led you to the shelf or the online link where you found this copy, or before someone who greatly cared for you handed this book to you, so you could journey this monumental part of your faith walk. I prayed that you would find these God-inspired words at just the right time in your life, as I wrote them at just the right time in mine.

Being *Open with Your Broken* is about addressing today's current crisis in faith through freedom, real freedom, and claiming the freedom that Jesus gives us from our past. You see, we are all sinners. Every single person walking the face of this earth comes with a plethora of sins. We all sin differently, varying in the how and when, but with one very simple common denominator that connects us all; our sin was taken to the cross with Jesus, and our debts were paid in full when He died.

Reading those words is one thing but accepting the freedom that the crucifixion of Jesus Christ offers to you, and the righteousness and grace you can freely receive proves to be one of the hardest struggles a believer will ever face. It is the actual acceptance of mercy and fulfillment of His grace. Through these chapters, you will begin to learn how Satan can use your past against you by causing feelings of guilt and shame.

Most importantly you will learn how once you claim power over your past and give glory to God in the transformation, you can use it to begin expanding His Kingdom, which leads me to the second thing you need to know. By the time you finish reading this book, you will know why it is so important to be open about the messiness of your past, no matter how ugly.

Today's generation of millennials is not identifying with any type of faith in disturbingly large numbers. There are bits and pieces of my own story that you may identify with or open your eyes to a walk you never knew. My transparency can share a perception about Christianity you weren't aware existed. Regardless of whether there is truth at the core of the millennial perception of today's Christian, the outcome is millions of young adults today are wading through life absent a relationship with Jesus Christ. That should be considered a serious faith crisis. In fact, Pew Research Center shows that over half of today's millennial generation view Christianity as judgmental. I strongly believe that stereotype would be challenged if the holier-than-now view of Christianity was challenged by transparent, honest believers, who talked about who they were *before* God got ahold of their hearts.

If believers were open about their mess, they would be less apt to fall into self-righteousness and walk in a grounded place of humility. Imagine meeting those who have yet to believe where they currently are, with the story of who you were, while delivering that message in a living testimony of God's transformative glory! Powerful right?

The good news is, whether you are beginning your walk as a believer, battling your past as a Christian, or trying to find out how to be more effective in expanding His Kingdom, you can find an answer *and* action within these words.

In the first chapter, I will unveil to you my own broken. It is all of my ugly, messy, past that I kept hidden from so many for so long because I was ashamed and afraid of judgment. Through the process I will share with you, you will see how God took me from the depths of despair—a broken woman full of sin and darkness—and transformed me into a woman full of faith, hope, and unwavering love for Jesus Christ. It is through that walk of faith that I have gained the knowledge, insight, and wisdom to help you on this very same journey.

I continue to tell everyone that I am a constant work in progress, and I thank God that He is not done with me yet! This is only one piece in my journey, but I am thankful that I can share such a monumental truth with so many who struggle with this paralyzing challenge. I am excited to journey this with you.

I pray that you will find your courage in Christ, to be open about your own past, and know that this world is not our home; it is only temporary. Those that you see around you—the people that you fear judgment from—matter not. It is our Lord and Savior who promises us no condemnation. He is the only One that we will stand before. Once you grasp that absolute truth, you are walking in the direction of true freedom.

At the beginning of each chapter, you will find a prayer. This prayer was specifically written for you to read before beginning that chapter. I encourage you to start each session of reading with the prayer that corresponds with the chapter you are reading. Inviting the Holy Spirit into this process is incredibly important and will make this journey much more impactful...so let's begin.

CHAPTER 1

My Own Broken

Father God,

Thank You for loving me, even when I fail to love myself. Thank You for allowing me this opportunity to read a transparent story of brokenness transformed by a loving, faithful God. Open my heart as I read these words, so that my mind and spirit are filled with Your purpose. Help me to see Your hand through every moment and allow me to hear Your voice amidst her story.

In Jesus' Holy Name I Pray, Amen.

It wasn't like I didn't know who God was. I mean, I attended Catholic mass intermittently with my grandmother, resulting in a weekly dose of religion add a hefty serving of guilt on the side. Who wouldn't want to sustain such invigorating rituals and repetition once breaking the mold of small-town life at eighteen years old? And aside from my painstaking religious humor, I would love to tell you that my broken began the day my parents dropped me off at college. However, years of "and how did that make you feel" therapy has taught me otherwise. In fact, there are three very important points I am going to tell you that are key to this entire book. One, we are all broken. Every single person walking the face of this earth is in some way, shape, or form, whether a little or a lot, broken. Two, some of this broken started long before you could ever even control the course of the crack—before you were even old enough to understand you were broken, before you could prevent it, or ever change it. Three, it is utterly amazing to be broken. It has been allowed with a higher reason, every crack, to create your *broken* in just the places necessary for you to fulfill your purpose.

So, now that you know we are all broken, and you know you are broken, I can share with you about my broken. That's how it seems to work right? We have to know first that we are in the company of others like us before we are comfortable with sharing ourselves. You see, all of this is really rooted in fear, and we will talk about this later in the chapter "Removing the Power from Your Past." However, that pause before we share a story, a testimony, a struggle, a sin, an addiction, even a prayer request is all rooted deeply in fear. Fear of being judged, fear of people not liking us, fear of being inadequate, fear, fear, fear. But as Christians, we *know* that fear is not of God. Fear not, we are told in His Word. We seem to forget this piece over and over again. Faith or fear, there is no room for both…so, *hi, my name is Dana, here is my broken*:

I think it is important for you to understand my beginning to appreciate the power of His transformation and the authenticity I bring to these words I write. I am not a biblical scholar, I do not know every Scripture in the Bible, and I am certain there are more than a few children's Bible stories that I would not be able to recite correctly.

However, what I write in this book, I have walked out in faith, studied, prayed over, will support with the truth found in His word, and wholeheartedly know that it is part of my purpose and calling to write it and to share with all of you reading it.

If I stood in front of you, you would find a thirty-something, tattooed, independent mother of two very active, biracial children. I have them twenty-four hours a day, seven days a week, and they are every bit a part of my strength, drive, purpose, and fire. Their stories are a part of my beautiful broken.

For years I chased love, there was an emptiness inside of me that sourced the depths of my broken. It had started out as a crack long before I could control the breaking, years before I knew I was broken. Yes, I knew right from wrong, was raised to do better, but I was a young girl, trying to fill a void, trying to feel secure in herself, with herself. Continued alcohol use was sprinkled with various drugs and sex, all while maintaining exceptional grades, exemplary test scores, a varsity athlete, finalized by acceptance into a rigorous collegiate honors program. I hid so much from my parents and thought I was hiding even more, from a God I knew of but didn't really know.

Once I went to college and could seek out ways to fill the emptiness absent a curfew, or parental disdain, the drug use increased and grew more severe. Thinking back, I'm honestly not sure how I survived. I barely remember my freshman year of college. I was in places that I should never have been, in situations I had only seen in movies, and with people I had known less than a few months.

Early into my sophomore year, I met an upperclassman. He had been recruited to our school to play soccer. He was straight-edged because of his athleticism, and I was like a chameleon, so he was good for my health in that regard. I quit all drug use and we only occasionally drank at various post-game parties. We dated, had a volatile two-year relationship, I got pregnant, and then we got married. Sounds like the fairy tale story you always read about, right?

Well, two years later, after marriage counseling, sustained emotional abuse, a host of other issues including infidelity on his part, I filed for divorce. We had been going to Church, for the sole purpose of having a Catholic wedding. I emphasize this because even though we were attending mass, there was no desire to grow a relationship of faith. It's as if it was just something we needed to do on Sunday to make sure we met the requirements the Church had set for us to get married there.

He was Catholic, I was raised Catholic, that's where we were married, went through our classes, etc. When I went to talk to the Priest about the divorce and everything that had transpired he simply looked at me and let me know there was a $532.00 filing fee to even consider it.

I was still in graduate school, and now raising my son on my own, and when I told him I couldn't afford it, I was told then maybe I'm not financially ready for divorce. I walked out of that church angry as if God himself just told me to continue dealing with everything I had been dealing with because I couldn't afford to pay him. I knew that wasn't how God worked, but after this, I was done with church.

Looking back, I was not *whole* in myself to enter into any partnership from the beginning, and that is a truth that took me years to realize. As much as I would love to blame my ex-husband for much of our breakdown, I was equally at fault. Swallowing the pill of accountability, tastes as awful as it felt.

Regardless, at the end of that situation, I left angry at the church, angry at God, let down by my ex-husband, and disappointed in myself. Now, I was a divorced, single mom, before the age of twenty-five. New cracks, stemming new brokenness.

I worked for the University while finishing my undergrad and raising my fantastic little guy. Classes were a breeze as academics always came naturally to me, but I was still devastatingly unhappy with how I looked. When I gave birth to my son, I was sixty pounds heavier than when I got pregnant. While we were still married, my [now] ex-husband made sure to publicly remind me of this regardless of who we were around or where we were.

To be honest, he was right, and I was too exhausted from a full-time job, full-time course schedule, and full-time toddler to do anything about it. But my insecurities with myself continued to deepen, and the thoughts in my head would remind me how disgusting I looked, questioning who would ever want me, and ensuring that I was destined for a life of solitude.

I met Frank while I was working on my Master's Degree. I had started my career as a Resident Director and began the Public Administration Program at the University. My son was three years old and in the pre-school program on campus. Most of my classes were in the evening, and a few were online, so I was able to balance my course schedule quite nicely. I took a few extra courses to receive my Graduate Certificate in Non-Profit Management and extended my program an additional year. We had met downtown, on one of my weekends off, at a local bar. His arm was broken, and he said he broke it playing recreational football at Western University. He was home on summer break but would be returning in the fall.

When I met Frank, I was pretty damaged. I didn't believe in the sanctity of marriage, had major trust issues, and incredibly low self-esteem. This doesn't sound like a recipe for success? He would tell me how beautiful I was in a way that made me think he was telling the truth. It had been years since I heard a man tell me that. I fell quickly for his words, his ability to make me feel good about myself, and paid little attention to his actions. Looking back, I am pretty certain Frank was the smoothest talker I had ever met.

As disaster number two began to unfold, I flew by every warning sign or red flag you can think of. I bought every excuse he came up with. When he didn't return to school in the fall because he wanted to re-evaluate his life plan, I somehow really understood and agreed that he shouldn't waste money if he wasn't sure of his career path. Well, go ahead and hit fast-forward a few years, twenty thousand dollars, a host of dramatic situations, and yes, another pregnancy. Add that to, a move to my hometown, a string of break-ups and get-back-togethers and we are almost through year two. Frank was arrested a few times, each of which I bailed him out, because God forbid the father of my child sits in jail, even though he was guilty every time.

I was brilliant in books, stellar in my career, but an absolute train wreck when it came to relationships. I mean seriously, even as I type this, I can only imagine what my family was thinking watching me drive the hot mess express also known as Dana's twenties.

Frank had become a closet alcoholic, minus the closet, and when I lost my career in my hometown, we moved back to the city where we had met. At that time our amazingly beautiful daughter was six months old. I had tried to get him to go to rehab four different times and kicked him out more often than that.

The truth is that I just didn't want to be the girl with two kids by two different dads. I was raised in a small town and had already broken the mold with interracial dating, then a divorce, and kids out of wedlock. I mean I was really setting the bar here. I don't know if I can explain to you how much longer that simple fear kept me tied to an unhealthy and damaging relationship.

When we moved back to Springfield, I had left him to unpack the first load of boxes, and I traveled back to my hometown to pack up the second load on the trailer and bring the kids. When I returned, He was gone, nothing unpacked, but beer boxes and empty liquor bottles were everywhere. After numerous calls, He showed up wasted, threw a drink in my face along with the key to the house and then disappeared for four days. I finally found him at a crack house, coming down off some sort of drug-induced binge. I remember sitting in my car with my daughter in the back seat as he was walking away and all I kept thinking to myself was how, how did I get to this place? I wish I could tell you that was the lowest point I reached in my broken, driving away with my daughter in the back seat and never looking back. He and I were over, but the depth of my broken certainly wasn't.

It was about eight months after the day I drove away. The kids were out of town with my sister, and I had just come in from a night out with my friends. As I laid down, I heard a knock at the front door. I assumed it was one of my girlfriends I had just been out with, so I quickly unlocked the door and opened it up. Frank bursts through telling me how important it is to check through the window before opening up the door for a stranger. He held me hostage in my house that night, threw me around, and when I broke free for my cell phone and tried to call the police he dragged me from one room to the next.

He finally got me down to the ground, shoved his knee into the back of my head, and wouldn't get up until I swore to comply. He flipped me over forcefully trying to kiss me as I fought him off, then he walked around bantering various threats and spouting slurs of hatred. He was high, drunk, and terrifying.

This went on for at least two hours before he stepped outside to smoke a cigarette. I army crawled across the floor to my laptop thinking if I could just get someone on Facebook to call the police since he had my cellphone, I could get help. He was watching through the window.

He came running in, grabbed my computer, threw me across the room, into the wall, and went back outside. He sat a chair directly in front of the screen door. I sat on the floor, tears streaming down my face. Inside I knew if I somehow didn't get out of this house he was going to rape me, kill me, or both.

I was sick to my stomach, and panic started to overwhelm me. I thought of my kids returning to the house, finding me dead, or allowing him to destroy me more than I had already given him access. That overwhelming panic turned to rage, and I slowly put on a pair of my sister's tennis shoes that were sitting next to the couch. I made as little movement as possible trying to not draw attention to myself. I slowly got up, and then sprinted to the door and kicked it as hard as I could. What I then thought was adrenaline strength, I now believe was Jesus. As he heard me come running, he went to stand up. I kicked the door into the chair, the chair flew into him, knocking him off the porch. I was able to escape and immediately started screaming and ran to the neighbors for help. He fled, I filed an order of protection and charges with the state's attorney.

He was arrested in a different county a few months later and then got heavy into drugs. For the next few years, I would keep tabs on him to make sure he was alive by checking his public record. He stayed in trouble so much that I knew he wasn't sober yet.

He convinced me once of his sobriety when our daughter was four years old. I took her to see him, he promised her an Easter basket that we were supposed to pick up two days later at his house, and then gave us a fake address to pick it up. She asked about that Easter basket until November, and every time she asked I would have to fight the fiercest hatred and pray for a heart to forgive. I refused to let him see her unless he got into an AA program or some sort of support group, so I knew he could be consistent and would have support through his recovery. He continues to choose otherwise.

Now during most of that time, I was on unemployment. Although I felt like I didn't have much to bring to the table, I met someone who thought the opposite. I know you are probably thinking the same thing my family was; girl, just sit down and take a break, you aren't good at this! My hard-headed resolve comes from my father's side, and I was still searching to fill an emptiness that I thought would be filled if I just found the right person.

Well, he was finishing his degree, and we dated for a few months before officially becoming a couple. He loved old cars and would buy, restore, and resell them as a hobby and part-time job while going to school. He also had children, and my love for him grew quickly. He was incredibly supportive of my struggle in finding a job, always encouraging, always positive. At the time he was an unexpected streak of light amidst a world of darkness. I was thankful.

I applied for more jobs than I can remember from a secretary to a loan analyst and everything in between. Wouldn't you know I was overqualified for nearly everything? I couldn't even get an interview because they said, they knew when something better came along I would take it, so they didn't want to invest time and energy into training me. At one point in Illinois, the unemployment had to be extended longer than usual, but there was a two-week time period in which we didn't know if that was going to happen. So many of us were unemployed in the nation, it was literally a nationwide crisis, and the federal government had to supplement unemployment assistance.

Well, in that two-week gap, my landlord served me with a five-day notice, not thinking that I was going to be able to make rent and not believing that they were going to extend our benefits. I was so offended I didn't even contact him. I was out in the five days, and my two kids and I moved into the bedroom of a great friend of mine who I consider a brother and his fiancé who is now his wife and their daughter until I could find an apartment for us. Plenty of amazing memories filled those months that I shared with my friends in that home. They were family, we were family, and in that time, we built a bond that became stronger than ever. In the same breath, there were moments that as a woman, raising children, I was overrun with shame, despair, and an overwhelming disappointment in myself. I was living, unemployed, with my two children, in the bedroom of someone else's home.

If I am truly going to be open with my broken than I will share the deepest depth of my "broken" within this testimony. Out of all the things I carried in my life, this was the heaviest, the hardest, and the most damaging. It was the burden that I carried all the way to the altar the day I got saved and baptized. It is what paralyzed me with fear when considering publishing this book. Yes, there were others that concerned me here and there, but this one was the one that I really needed to feel God's mercy, this was the one that I feared worldly judgment from. This is where I can see the shared perspective of over half of the millennials who believe Christians are judgmental.

The day I was moving out of the house and into my friend's house I got a horrible pain and had been rushed to the ER. It turned out that not only did I have a kidney stone, something that was common for me since I was fourteen years old, but I also found out that I was pregnant, with what would have been my third child.

Yes, I was on birth control and using protection. When the nurse uttered those words, I felt like the world around me came crashing down. Time stopped, life was turned over, and this thought now consumed me. Although I loved the man I was with, I was mortified that I found myself in such a juvenile situation at my age. We were not reckless or irresponsible, but still, I found myself facing those consequences. Fear was all that consumed me. I was moving into the bedroom of someone else's home, no real income, no job leads, and had two children that I was already struggling to provide for. He was only my boyfriend, not my husband, and quite honestly, the track record so far would lead me to believe I would be raising a third on my own at some point in time.

I was sickened by the thought of an abortion and haunted by any other option. I was destroyed by my own debates I had given in high school that adamantly supported pro-life and demanded that people only understand that point of view. Here I found myself in a situation, abandoned from faith, absent from hope, and all I knew at that time was that I could not feasibly bring another child into this situation that I had created for my family. And I was too ashamed to even discuss other options, I didn't want anyone to know. It was selfish and prideful.

There was no one that I called or talked to. I was too embarrassed and ashamed to talk to my family. I know many people who have never been in this situation would say, well why didn't you choose adoption? I used to be one of those people. All I can say is this; fear drove every ounce of my thought process. Fear of judgment, fear of the unknown, fear consumed me. It's as if I was in a fog and I had two options. I had convinced myself that having a baby wasn't one. He was supportive of my decision, and although it contradicted his, he allowed it to be my own.

I remember driving an hour away to the facility and was met with protestors who screamed things as I pulled in. They yelled things like *murderer* and said I was *going to burn in hell*. Each sign had some symbol of Christianity on it—a cross, the fish. They had signs. I had tears.

Once inside I sat and waited for what seemed like an eternity. There were a few other women, various ages. We all sat in somber silence. When they called my name, the process began, they verified that I was just a few weeks along, and then I took a few pills, read some instructions, filled out forms, and a short while later was driving home to the sound of silence only broken by my uncontrollable crying.

I laid in bed for what felt like days. I didn't want to take any pain meds. I wanted to endure the pain. I wanted some sort of punishment. I was different after that, everything in me had changed. I was darker, hurt by my own actions, sad that I had come to this place in my life. I knew I had to hide from God. I had done the worst, they had shouted it, burn in hell. It was a pivotal part of my broken. The deepest part by far.

The next month when I took my son to register for school, reality knocked me down once again. Because I was living with another family and did not have my own address, they registered our family as homeless. I walked out of his school, sat in my car and cried. How did I get to this place? I remember asking myself that question as I sat with my daughter a year earlier, and yet I would gladly rewind the clock to that place rather than this one, a homeless murderer.

I felt like this was all punishment. I was falling deeper into this hole of despair, of darkness. It was too much, and in looking back I would like to think that I prayed, but I didn't. I knew of God but was terrified to turn to Him because of the sins I carried.

I remembered trying to go to church after my divorce even after being angry with the Priest. With my son on my hip and no ring on my finger, I remember the judgment I received in that church that morning. I was in college, our divorce wasn't final, but I just needed to be uplifted and the judgment I was given from the people around me who had no idea what storm I was in, cast me so far away from that place I swore to never go back—and I never did. And now…*murderer*, they screamed it at me. I had no place in His house. I didn't have the guts to even say His name out loud. I just cried. It was the loneliest time in my life.

When I looked at other Christians, they all had it together; they portrayed this life of togetherness. I was the farthest thing from that. I had no business turning to God with what I had done, with who I was. He was angry with me, I knew it, burn in hell, they told me my judgment, and I accepted it with defeat.

It took a couple of months, but I finally found a place that would accept my unemployment as income. It was a one-bedroom, very small apartment, in a location they called the mini-trenches. It was located on the west side of the city, but this specific complex was run down and known for crime. We didn't have any other choice, and so the kids got the bedroom, and I moved my bed into the back of the living room. My boyfriend and I decided to live together, not that we had reached that place as a couple, but financially it would benefit us both.

For the next year, we dealt with shootings, drug addicts banging on our door, and not knowing how we were going to make ends meet. My relationship became unstable, and I began questioning everything I thought I had known. There were times when I looked in the cabinets and there was enough for the kids to eat and that was it.

My son was old enough to know life was different; he knew not to ask for things at the store like he used to. They weren't allowed to play outside because it wasn't safe. Life for us was dramatically different; it was scarier, harder, everything was less than before. My parents would help me when they could, they would bail me out of this bill or that bill, but they had bills of their own and I felt shameful every time I had to call and ask. I had a stack of rejection letters, one hundred and thirty-two to be exact and those were just the ones that came by mail. All of which were thanking me for my interest but regretting to inform me I was overqualified for the position that I had applied for and it had been filled by another candidate. I never thought my degrees would prevent me from getting a job. My daughter's daycare cost alone would be twice as much as my monthly rent.

It was spring and most of the nation was still unemployed. They were calling us 99'rs because we were nearing our 99th week of unemployment. The extensions had been made and the government had made the decision they were not going to extend unemployment anymore. I broke down once again.

I picked up the phone and called my mom. "Mom, I don't know what I can do, I have tried everything possible, I apply to everything I can every week, but there is nothing. No one will even give me an interview. They aren't going to extend my benefits. I have four weeks left. If I don't get a job, we will have nothing." I was sobbing. My mom was always a spiritual person, but in her own way, not in formal religious ways and she never spoke about it with us.

Most of our religious upbringing came through my grandparents. That's why I was so surprised when my mom very simply said, "Honey, just give it up to God. Your aunt gave me this book, and it is about coming to the end of your own means, and when you reach that point, when there is nothing more you can do, you just have to release it to God. Literally Dana, you need to just look up to Him, lift your hands up in the air and tell Him to take it. Tell Him that you can't do it on your own and you need Him to take it. He will."

I sat there thinking, oh but mom, you don't know what I've done. Who I actually am. If she only knew the darkness inside her daughter on the other end of the phone, I am certain she would not be saying this to me. I struggled in my mind, but to her, I simply said okay. She told me I would be okay and gave me more amazing mom comfort words of love and strength. She has always been one of the most empowering women I have ever known.

As I hung up the phone, I immediately felt the pit in my stomach and my mind began to flood with guilt. How dare you turn to God now when you need help, do you think He's forgotten about the things you have done? Only this time, instead of allowing those thoughts to stop me, and imㅡㅡㅡㅌ me, I listened to my mom. I didn't know what else to do.

So, as foolish as I felt, and as ashamed as I was, tears started to pour from my eyes. In my one-bedroom apartment in the mini-trenches, on my knees in the middle of my living room floor, in all of my darkness, carrying the weight of my sins, I lifted my hands to my ceiling… "God, I cannot do this on my own. I am so sorry for everything I have done. I know you are mad at me, all I can say is I am so sorry, please forgive me, God, I need you to help me. Take this; I can't do it anymore."

As I dropped my hands, I cried the deepest most soul-cleansing cry I had cried in years. I buried my face in my carpet and just laid on the floor, I was exhausted, but a restful peace had come over me in place of the anxiety that I had before. I can't describe it, but I wasn't fearful or full of shame like I thought I would be.

The very next day, I am going to repeat this, the very next day, I received two phone calls from two different places offering me interviews and an email offering me a third. I immediately called my mom screaming on the phone. But for me, it was much bigger than just an interview for a job. This moment was me realizing that God was not so angry with me that I was condemned forever. I had accepted a judgment that man placed on me, not God, and because of that I ran from Him and tried to do life without Him making my life harder and darker and lonelier than it had to be. The moment I called out to Him, there He answered. My heart was bursting that I was not damned forever. And that moment, that day that God met me there on my living room floor, began the very small steps towards losing everything I knew about religion and building my relationship with Jesus Christ.

I was offered a great job with a non-profit and a few months later I was offered an even greater job utilizing my Public Administration Master's Degree in state government. When I applied for it, I called it my dream job!

I continued working both positions part-time for the non-profit and full time with the government. Although the sixty-hour weeks were difficult, it kept my mind off the heartbreak I was enduring after finding out I fell in love with another Mr. Wrong who was having another relationship with a woman for about six months. Devastated would be an understatement, but he moved out, and I threw myself into my work and building the world back up to where it once was for my kids.

All summer he was trying to work things out and although history would tell me otherwise, when your heart is hungry it will eat lies. I think one of the hardest battles we face sometimes is between our heart and mind. Now I have learned to cross-reference my thoughts and desires with the

Word of God, align is proceed, not aligned is a no-go. Back then, my heart always seemed to win the battle but lose the war.

By the end of the summer, I had saved enough money to move from that one-bedroom apartment into a three-bedroom townhouse and catch up on all things that were left financially outstanding. Look at God!

About one week before we were to move into the new townhouse I had been praying for, I was driving home from work and returning his calls about dinner plans. He had been talking about a house out in the country he wanted to buy and trying to convince me to not sign on the townhouse. It had great space for the kids and a garage for him to fix his old cars.

Every ounce of me wanted to believe it, and I was falling. He was not giving up on proving to me that he wanted a second chance at our relationship. My heart was slowly winning the battle over my mind, not knowing that I was about to experience the most disastrous, traumatic, and life-changing course of events that I had ever been a part of.

Without going into detail, he had been arrested and charged with a host of criminal charges. There was a federal unit, yes, an entire unit, looking for me for questioning about these charges and had been to several houses in town that I had previously lived. I was confused, scared, angry and hurt. In one day, my entire world, the reality I existed in had been turned upside down, shaken, ransacked (literally) and left for me to pick up the pieces.

Women came out of the woodwork that he had been seeing on the side. In the end, he was sentenced to twenty-five years in prison, and it would take me a few years before I let go of the anger, bitterness, and mounds of betrayal before I was finally able to write him, accept his apology, walk out the true meaning of grace, and embrace closure. But that will come in another book.

That situation did not break me; I was shattered. It was as if a bomb had detonated in the most sacred place of my trust, loyalty, and love. All I was left with was pieces scattered everywhere and I had no desire to put anything back together. I remember sitting in a counselor's office a week after it all happened. My family doctor wouldn't let me leave without speaking to someone and physically walked me down to see her. I stared at the wall, thoughtless, but filled with pain. I said to the woman, if this is what it feels like when a woman loses her spouse, then I do not ever want to be in love again. And I meant it.

I walked around like a zombie, numb, for weeks. I heard others in the office talking about it as it made headlines, and I simply kept my head down, running to the bathroom to hide my tears.

It would take an invitation to church, and indebtedness to Christ, that would truly save me from myself. You see, my entire everything was nearly lost in my eyes, and as if Jesus dying on the Cross for me was not enough, Him rescuing me from that situation, keeping us at arm's length and under His faithful protection, made me feel indebted to Him in a way that was real in the present tense. It was bigger than the mercy He had for me; it was purpose. I realized that He saved me for a reason, and not only was I able to be forgiven from the depths of my sin, but that I was able to be used.

I began reading Scripture regularly, thirsting after His word, His guidance, His presence. I started attending a church that was different than any other place I had ever experienced. The people were authentic and kind. It was *home* the moment I walked in and I felt God's presence every Sunday. They offered small groups, Bible study class, and Praise and Worship Nights. I attended everything. I soaked it all up as if I were finding water for the very first time after walking the sands of the desert for decades. Every drink was better than the last, refreshing, refueling, and I couldn't stop drinking from the well of Christ. A year later, I was baptized at this very same church. In that moment, my freedom began.

You see, we all have a story. Not everyone will have one as broken as mine, some will be more, some will be different, but we are all different sinners thankful for the same Cross.

I can tell you that I never thought that I would be courageous enough or free enough in my faith with Christ to share those broken moments with the world in a book. But what I have learned is this… my freedom is through

Christ. All those things that I shared in this chapter doesn't encompass all of my sin. There are plenty of times I was angry or gossiped, cursed, or was jealous and bitter. I physically fought a few times and drank way too much. These are the moments that I carried with me that I felt condemned, these are the cracks that deviated from my path, my journey, my walk. These are the pieces of my past that the enemy preyed on and played with, using in his schemes against me to keep me from God.

The truth is that Jesus saw all these things when He hung on that Cross, even the things I have yet to do, and He still chose me. The most beautiful, amazing, powerful moment in the history of the world is that He looked at your sin too, all of it, everyone's, and He chose each and every one of us despite it all. So, there is nothing that you have done, there is no story that you can share, there is no mess in your past, present, or future, that Jesus hasn't already seen and said, "I still choose you!" That is the power of the Cross. And that is why I am free to share my story and be open with my broken, because it brings glory to God and who He is as our Redeemer! The same is true for your story as well. That is powerful.

That is Jesus Christ.

CHAPTER 2

Removing the Power from Your Past

Father God,

Thank You for choosing me. Thank You for loving me with such amazing purpose and unconditional, powerful love that I cannot possibly describe it with worldly terms. Thank You for sending Your Son, Jesus Christ to pay our ransom in full so that our sins may be forgiven through Him and our salvation in Heaven secure. Prepare my heart as You speak to me through these words and move in my Spirit to grow closer to You, Father God.

In Jesus' Mighty Name I Pray, Amen.

Being open with your broken is much more than just owning what you have done and talking to Jesus about it. Because as much as Jesus knew everything you were going to do before you did it, the enemy knew everything you did as you were doing it.

Let's think about that for a second. You mean, Jesus knew that I was going to make some big mistakes in my life? Yes. God knew I was going to journey that entire first chapter plus some, and yet still seeing the sin of the world in all of us, our individual chapter ones, God still sent His son to die for us.

Jesus, to know that He was saving the world from death, including those who were putting Him to death, He still suffered and died anyway. Incredible, right? I mean, it is still hard for me sometimes to really fathom that kind of love and mercy. Now, the other side of that statement I made was that the enemy knew of your sin as you were committing it.

See, sometimes people put Satan and God on the same plane as if they are on equal but opposite ends of the spectrum. That is so far from being the truth, I mean, the only truth to that is God is light, and the enemy is darkness. The point to understanding that they are not equal in any way is because God is omnipresent, He is everywhere at all times. He can see in the future, and because of the Holy Spirit within us, He can hear our thoughts, our prayers, our worries, even those that don't form words.

Satan simply studies us, with a host of demons set out to do the same. They watch our reactions to see what pleases our flesh, what our temptations are, because as Jesus tell us in (John 10:10), the enemy (the thief) comes only to steal, kill and destroy. Satan is watching when you commit sin and keeps a record of your wrong. He is the master of deception, fear, guilt, and shame.

This is crucial to your understanding because the guilt of our sins is one of the most powerful attacks the enemy uses against us. Let me repeat that, the guilt and shame of your past sin, even if it was yesterday, is one of the most powerful attacks the enemy will use to keep us from receiving the grace of Christ and experiencing the true freedom of living out His righteousness.

You may be wondering how this can be, if we know we are forgiven in Christ Jesus, then how can this be such a powerful attack from the enemy? Well, because many Christians confuse condemnation from the enemy as conviction from God. They feel that God is upset with them, disappointed, or that it is God reminding them of the things they have done, shaming them for their sins. It feels real, the pit in their stomach, the shame of their actions, or the thoughts in their mind. It all exists, it is present, and there is nothing you can do to rewind that clock; so, you are simply stuck with the consequence, and that is the prime playground for the enemy.

You are probably now at this moment thinking about times that this has happened to you. That was not God, not one time, and it is important for you to not only equip yourself from attacks in the future but to help other Christians who may struggle with these very issues. Trust me when I tell you, this is an issue that every single Christian battles with at some point, at many points, or for some throughout the entirety of their walk with Christ.

In the first chapter, I spoke about how I was certain that God was angry with me, and the moment I would lean toward God, my mind would fill with shameful, guilt-filled thoughts. Every single time that happened it was the enemy in my head.

How do I know that? Because God doesn't work in the business of condemnation and He makes that very clear through the letters of His Apostle Paul, in the Book of Romans. He doesn't try to shame people away from Him. Romans 8:1 begins with a powerful statement of truth, "there is therefore now no condemnation for those who are in Christ Jesus. For the law of the Spirit of life has set you free in Christ Jesus from the law of sin and death."

Now, you could be thinking, but I wasn't *in* Christ when I was sinning, and I wasn't *in* Christ when I was trying to come back to the Lord. In fact, I wasn't *in* faith at all. It wasn't until I messed it all up that I started knocking on the door asking if I could come in. So how would this even apply to me?

In the Gospel of Luke chapter 15, we find Jesus Himself speaking in three different parables, all relating to sinners who have come back to God and how God accepts them and rejoices when they are found.

The first is the Sheppard who loses one of His sheep, and He carries that sheep on His shoulders once He finds Him and rejoices over the one lost but now found more-so than the ninety-nine that were never lost. He then speaks of a woman who loses a coin and searches her entire house for the coin she has lost and once found calls all of her neighbors and friends to rejoice over finding it because it is of such value to her.

The last is the Parable of the Prodigal Son and the one that means the most to me because I feel I relate to it so very much. The Parable starts in Luke Chapter 15 verse 11, about a man with two sons.

The father has two sons. One decides he wants his inheritance now. This request in itself is incredibly disrespectful, but still, the father gives his son his share of the money. After receiving it, the son leaves and spends it living a wild life filled with sin and debauchery. He finds himself so low he is hired to feed hogs and eventually desires the very food the swine are eating. The rebellious son comes to his senses and decides to return home to ask his father if he would hire him. As he returns, the father sees his son and runs to him, forgiving him instantly and throwing a feast for his return. The son that never rebelled is angry about the celebration of his rebellious brothers return to the father. The father explains his joy for his "prodigal" son has returned.

The point to all of this is, if you seek Christ, you will receive Him, and if you receive Christ, you will be in Christ and for those who are in Christ Jesus there is no condemnation. Jesus taught these parables to show us this with specific purpose. More so than that, God tells us the value we are to Him even after we have gone astray. In Luke 15:7, Jesus says, "In the same way, I tell you that there will be more joy in heaven over one sinner who repents than over ninety-nine righteous ones who do not need to repent."

There is joy when you come back to God. Do you think then that it would be God in your head reminding you of everything you've done wrong, or telling you that you are not worthy to step foot in His house, hearing an inner voice condemn you as a hypocrite? Would God do that if the entire heavens rejoice over one sinner who repents more than ninety-nine righteous? Clearly we see the truth in the Word that condemnation does not come from God. The enemy, however, will surely condemn you to keep you from Christ. Because as long as we are walking without God, we are not useful to the Kingdom, and that is just as good for Satan.

Discerning the difference between conviction and condemnation and accepting God's forgiveness and grace is what will embark you on a journey of true freedom. Breaking the bondage of your past is knowing that when Jesus took your sins to the cross, it was finished. When Jesus was on the Cross, before committing His Spirit to His Father, He literally said in John 19:30, "It is finished." The translation isn't just finished as in, this crucifixion is done. No, this finished is from the Greek word *tetelestai*, which translated means it is accomplished, or it has been completed. Jesus is talking about salvation of the world, the prophecy coming to fruition, and full resolution of sin.

The crucifixion of Jesus Christ was one of the most horrendous, torturous, unjust acts of all time. Jesus was sinless, blameless, and walked only in love and light. He walked in a fallen world, flooded with sin, and the only way to ensure our salvation was to release bondage from the old law, and pay our ransom for salvation. God wasn't going to rebuke His law just because people decided to go against it.

Instead, God worked within His law, using the perfect sacrifice, His Son, to not only die for us but to eradicate the old law with a new covenant. It is the blood of Jesus Christ that redeems us, that allows us to be forgiven, and it is the covenant that allows us to ascend into Heaven with the Lord, Jesus, the angels, and all the fellow believers who have passed on before us. What an amazing finish line at the end of our marathon, right?

So, if God did not truly forgive you when you sought forgiveness through Jesus Christ, that would be saying that the bloodshed of His Son was not worthy enough. As if something you could do on this earth is bigger than His own Son being tortured, crucified, and dying on the Cross for the sole purpose of our salvation.

If you have a child, or even a niece or nephew, someone that you love more than life itself, that is of your own flesh and blood, imagine giving their life for someone else's. What kind of life would you want that person to have considering someone you loved tremendously died so they could live it?

Now take it a step further, imagine if your loved one died willingly and with purpose, so this other person could be forgiven and be allowed to live in your house. The only stipulation is that they have to believe that it is your house and ask you for forgiveness when they mess up. What would your forgiveness look like for that person, knowing someone you loved so immensely gave their life to allow them forgiveness and into your house? Puts God's forgiveness into perspective, right?

Salvation through Christ, mercies new each morning, those are promises given to us by God. Your confession of sin to Him, and your desire for His forgiveness in your heart equates to His mercy. Sins wiped away leaving you as white as snow. That mercy, that type of real forgiveness, we aren't familiar with in our flesh. We carry it around much longer than we should, not because God hasn't forgiven us, He tells us in His word He has, but rather we struggle with accepting His forgiveness and receiving His grace because we aren't used to giving it to others, receiving it from others, or offering it to ourselves. It is hard to understand something that you aren't used to, and the enemy knows that and uses that over and over again.

At the beginning of this chapter, I brought up the letter from Paul in Romans and how impactful it is for anyone seeking to truly understand the extent of God's grace. The beginning of Romans Chapter 8 will prove to be one of the most powerful promises for you to stand on during this journey of removing any power that lies in your past. I want to revisit this Scripture from Paul again. He is writing to believers and *encouraging* them, so it is evident that even thousands of years ago Christians were struggling with the acceptance of God's grace. This isn't a new battle we are facing here folks. "Therefore, there is now no condemnation for those who are in Christ Jesus, because through Christ Jesus the law of Spirit who gives life has set you free from the law of sin and death." Let's reflect on the freedom that lies in that promise from God.

Therefore, there is now no condemnation for those who are in Christ Jesus.

That means as a believer, if you believe Jesus Christ died on the Cross with your sins, there is no condemnation for you. None!

Condemnation is from the Latin word *condemnare*, which means to sentence, blame, or disapprove. God is telling His followers that there is no sentence, no judgment, no blame set on those who believe in Him, for the law of the Holy Spirit who gives you life, sets you free from the sins of your past and the judgment of death. When Christ took our sins on the Cross, He didn't take some of them, He didn't take all the sins for just some of us, and He didn't pay our ransom in part.

He took ALL the sin, for ALL the world, and paid the ransom for us in FULL. What is left up to us, is choosing Him. What we get in return, is His mercy, grace, forgiveness, love, righteousness, and so many other amazing gifts unique to a relationship with Christ.

For many I have talked to in preparation for writing this book and journeying my walk of faith, I would say they compared starting a relationship with Christ to getting a new car. It's new, feels good, needs to be shiny on the outside, needs to look different so others can see that it is different, and a host of other appearance factors.

Those were assumptions about faith, not the truth. They placed far too much concern about what others thought instead of who they were building a relationship with! God doesn't call us to be *shiny*, or even appear to be, and Jesus didn't tell us to follow other Christians. His exact words, found in Matthew 16:24, Jesus said to his disciples, "Whoever wants to be my disciple must deny themselves and take up their cross and follow me." Wow!

Deny yourself, deny the world, don't worry about what they think, know that you will face some faith-pains (your Cross) and follow Him. Jesus met people in the depths of their despair, and never once asked His disciples to clean up their appearance before sharing the good news.

God is much more concerned with what is happening within your heart and mind, than the world's opinion of how you look, or what they think. I mean Jesus Himself wasn't concerned with what religious leaders thought when He was preaching at the watering wells or eating among the tax collectors. Jesus loves broken people because we are all broken people. The biggest fallacy about Christianity today is that you can't step inside a church until you have it together, because the people that you would be sitting around have it together. False, super false.

I will be the first to tell you, I was one of those people who used to think that, and it kept me from the amazing church I now call home for years. This thought is from the enemy and it is fed to people to keep them out of the house of God, stopping them from hearing His truth, developing relationships with fellow believers, and walking out their purpose!

If the enemy can keep you in shame about what you have done and feeling inadequate about your current situation he can keep you out of the very place you need to be. The truth is that the church is a hospital for the broken, a fellowship of sinners all celebrating their need and thankfulness for the same Cross.

Every single person is a work in progress; thank God for that! A mind that is stuck in the world cannot possibly begin to believe, let alone fully accept the amazing things that God has in store for us, or all that is offered through a relationship with Him.

Most importantly accepting the mercy and grace that was given through Christ's sacrifice on the Cross. "And do not be conformed to this world but be transformed by the renewing of your mind so that you may prove what the will of God is, that which is good and acceptable and perfect" (Romans 12:2).

Quite honestly, the only thing comparable to a new car purchase when starting a relationship with Christ is that many Christians, although forgiven of their past, still take all of their sin from the trunk of the old car and load it into the trunk of the new car, ignoring the mercy, grace, and forgiveness that is freely given to them.

Now, I am not saying you are supposed to forget that it ever existed or fail to remember the life lessons that came with it. No, what I am saying is that you are not supposed to be filled with shame, guilt, and embarrassment once you have accepted Christ and asked for forgiveness. So many believers really struggle with accepting forgiveness for themselves, from a past that they cannot change. In an article entitled "The Dark Side of Being Light," Robin Lee calls this our Shadow Self. It is the dark side of our past that can cause shame, guilt, and condemnation if we allow it to. Many times, as we draw closer to the light, it is our darkness, our shadow self, that seems to grow if we leave it unaddressed.

This is a huge challenge for Christians! We struggle with truly embracing the forgiveness and mercy that Christ gives to us. Why? Because it is not in our worldly logic to comprehend. We cannot fathom that type of forgiveness, because we rarely give it to others as easily as it says it is given to us. We aren't offered it in this world as Jesus offers it, and quite frankly even if we have experienced the first two, we fail miserably at offering to forgive ourselves. Have you ever said, I've beaten myself up over it, or I will never forgive myself? That is exactly what the enemy wants because where we do not allow forgiveness to enter, becomes the playground for torment, shame, guilt, and a barrier to grow in our faith.

Forgiveness

Forgiving myself would prove to be one of my biggest battles that I faced as a Christian. It was a do not trespass sign standing in the way of my growth with Jesus Christ. For years I struggled with anger, bitterness, and other worldly feelings all attached to things that I carried inside. I didn't want to forgive myself specifically for the abortion because I didn't want to remove the gravity of what I had done, or make light of it, and I didn't want God to think that I wasn't really sorry.

God, the One who created me, did not need to see me beat myself up or hide from Him to know I was truly sorry. It's just like when your Mom knows if you are genuinely sorry about something, she just knows. She knows you, and God knows each of us. This was something I had to learn when offering forgiveness to other people. God didn't want me to earn His forgiveness, I asked, I was sorry in my heart and I was forgiven. We are told in Scripture to forgive others as He forgives us, but how often do we expect others to show us that they are sorry, "prove it" we might say. God doesn't really work like that and I don't think He honors our forgiveness process when we do either.

Moving on from this thought process was two-fold. One, I had to start making peace with people that I had yet to forgive. I seriously had to search my soul to let go of anything, and I mean *anything* that I could have possibly been holding onto that I needed to forgive others for. I started a forgiveness journal, yes, a forgiveness journal. I know it sounds like it made the top ten reject list for activities during vacation bible school, but sometimes we must break it down to simple processes to get the end result we need.

So, I would pray and ask God to help me search my soul, my heart, and my mind for things that I needed to let go of, people I needed to forgive, situations that were still casting some sort of stronghold on my heart. I prayed that He would help reveal these to me so that I could begin to forgive. I encourage everyone reading this book, if you have yet to pray that type of prayer, even if you don't think you have people that you haven't forgiven, pray it! You will be amazed at the depths of which stuff can get buried!

As my well of *unforgiven* began to unravel, I wrote about how I felt and why I was forgiving each person. At the end of each one, I prayed for that person and asked for Jesus to help me truly offer that forgiveness in my own heart. Talk about a spiritual cleansing!

I understand that some people may get to the end of that last sentence and think, yea that sounds great and all but that's too much of a process, a little too hokey pokey for me. I again will tell you, growing your faith is discipline, it's like learning or mastering anything. There are steps and maneuvers that you must learn or lessons you need to go through that build your foundation. It's the general education curriculum before you can get to your coursework in completing your degree.

Praying with God regarding unforgiveness in your heart is a crucial part of the foundation, and even if it doesn't quite vibe with you, God will honor your discipline. Walk through the steps to get you to the freedom you deserve to have.

Now, as many will find, there were a few situations and/or people that took a little more than just a paragraph on a page and a prayer to get to the place of real forgiveness. When I talk about forgiveness, I don't mean the arms crossed—*I forgive you for being a jerk*—type of acceptance. I mean truly empathizing with the situation to soften your heart and really offer forgiveness. Sin isn't weighted in God's eyes, and the wrongs that were done to you, you most certain have done to others in some form or fashion. Remove your pride, focus on Jesus, and really forgive.

Now trust me when I say, I know this is difficult; remember I walked out this entire book before writing it. The very first article published in *The Praying Woman* was about me embarking on this very process, "Forgiveness Isn't Always a One-Shot Deal," that details my struggle with forgiving my daughter's dad. In the end, a lengthy process that started with a forgiveness journal, reached a status of empathy, and then a heart of true forgiveness which only our Savior could provide.

I will share that process with you as it was pivotal in my faith walk. You see, one of the greatest gifts we are given as followers of Christ is grace. For a moment, I want you to picture Jesus Christ on the Cross. Blood, sweat, and tears encompass this pivotal crucifixion. He bared the weight of our sins, even the ones we don't know we will commit yet, and still, He chose us anyway. He chose YOU anyway. He chose ME anyway. Despite our past, present, and future, He chose love and covered us in the truest form of forgiveness: grace.

The power of God's grace is immeasurable, in fact, I am certain that we have yet to find a combination of words that even begins to scratch the surface of its power. Amazing, right? Thinking about the grace we receive is this beautiful, smile-inducing, deep exhale reassuring, faith lift. Yet, most of us, when we think about the grace we give to others normally stirs up a different set of internal reactions. Christians who are struggling with the forgiveness of others is less like the thirty-something sheepish single, requesting a table for one, and more like a sold-out Adele concert with an exponentially long wait list. So, the good news is, you aren't alone, but why is grace the most amazing to receive, but at times a seriously challenged offering?

There are times that I am fantastic at forgiveness! When a person is genuinely sorry, when I know their intentions were not to upset or harm, when it was accidental, insignificant, or a fleeting moment of an understandable situation, in those moments, my forgiveness game rivals Steph Curry on the court! But what about those other moments, when a person really hurts you or even worse hurts someone you love? When they aren't sorry or won't take responsibility for their actions to even begin to be sorry? That is where the "challenged offering" of forgiveness for many comes into play. God makes it pretty clear how we are to handle forgiveness throughout Scripture.

Matthew 5:7 says, "Blessed are the merciful, for they will be shown mercy." Colossians 3:13 says, "Bear with each other and forgive one another if any of you has a grievance against someone. Forgive as the Lord forgave you." There are a variety of other Scriptures where the Lord calls us to forgive as we have been forgiven and that we will be given mercy as we have been merciful to others. I really don't to face God and His mercy with my mess ups, sins, and failures takes as long to receive as the mercy I have given others. If that is the case, my pearly gate wait time will rival the DMV. But, in all seriousness, like many others, I have struggled with forgiving numerous times, and it is a battle that I still face from time to time in different situations. But overcoming one of my biggest battles of forgiveness is what really gave me the desire to aid others who may be stuck in a place of saying they have forgiven, but not feeling that they forgave.

My daughter is nine. She is a beautiful, amazing, brilliant, sassy creation of our King, and I am blessed to call myself her mom. Her dad has been non-existent most of her life after struggling with drug addiction since she was eight months old. I spent two years making a substantial effort to create some type of consistent, safe, and healthy relationship for them but after numerous broken promises, question-filled evenings, and a tear streaked little girl, I stopped, and thus so did any type of relationship.

The simple thought of him filled me with rage. Over the next three years, I received random inebriated phone calls claiming sobriety or transformation, each one filled with more lies than the one before. I would spew the most hateful, venomous words that even I didn't know I was capable of saying. I shook with anger and whatever forgiveness I had told myself I had given him since the last phone call was long gone. I would hang up the phone and every time feel defeated. Battle lost, he had won, and not her father, I knew it was the enemy. How do you forgive someone who continues to cause pain? Who is not even sorry? How do you forgive that?

Well, although I had thought I had given it to God before, I think I took it back quite a few times. This time I truly gave it to God; I was exhausted, overly consumed, and tired of being angry. I wanted to forgive Him because I didn't want to carry it, not because I felt he deserved it. I am blessed to have a great Pastor friend who often helps me navigate through some of the tougher avenues of faith. I reached out to him through this struggle, and his advice through this battle was this… "Forgiveness is not always a one-time shot. There are going to be times that you may have to forgive and wake up tomorrow and forgive again."

That was new to me. I guess I hadn't really ever thought about forgiveness as a process but more as an action. I would love to get to a place where I can simply forgive, and it boom, be an action, done. It's just this pasty stuff that covers my body. God calls it flesh, and yea, I struggle with it. So, still I was concerned and replied, "But what if I don't even want to forgive him? I only know that I am supposed to forgive him." And He said to me, "Then start praying to God to prepare your heart to *want* to forgive him. Baby steps, Dana, sometimes we have to get there through baby steps, and forgiveness is not exempt from that." God is so merciful that He knows we are not, well Him. The desire in our hearts should be to reflect Him as closely as possible. God knows you aren't going to be able to forgive every situation with as much ease as He forgives us when we seek it. If you desire a heart of forgiveness, you know God will transform that in you. It is within His will, that's an easy one!

So, I started to talk to God about it in the most transparent conversation I think I've ever had. I was honest with my feelings, with my anger, with my fears. I knew God knew all of it, He had witnessed everything that had been done, but talking to Him about it was a different release for me. I asked Him to help prepare my heart, so I could eventually want to forgive her dad. Now, I am not going to tell you that I woke up the next morning and wanted to forgive him, because I didn't. I had to continue praying for this preparation and it took quite a few months. Over time, I started gaining compassion for him, not justifying his actions, but I honestly started seeing her dad through the eyes of Jesus. I saw him as a lost son of Christ, and my anger turned to sadness.

Through the forgiveness process, the journaling, searching my soul, digging up stuff, and working on making a challenged offering a task with more ease, God was preparing my heart. He was conditioning it, helping me to understand in a very small way a sliver of the mercy we are given through Jesus and what He did for us on the Cross. I struggled to accept it before because I wasn't offering it.

Once I started living forgiveness with others, I could understand the forgiveness that was offered to me. Understanding God's forgiveness is huge, seriously HUGE, in your journey. I mean, you read the first chapter, right? So, you can see how major it was for my journey! Even if your journey isn't as messy as mine, or maybe it's messier, regardless, it is important to know as a Christian that Jesus covered it all.

At some point you are going to meet someone who doesn't understand the beauty and amazing-ness of this pivotal key to catapulting their relationship with Christ. You might be sitting next to the *me* in the Sanctuary, who needs someone to walk her through with truth and love instead of religion. I want you to bookmark this in your mind, ingrain it, study it, remember it, accept it and be ready to revisit it in the last chapter!

Now, I am not going to assume that just because you have begun forgiving others or reading about it and now understand the correlation between living forgiveness and receiving God's forgiveness for yourself that this automatically gets you to a place of receipt. If only it were that easy, right?

However, what I will tell you is that you are moving in the right direction. This is not a potion, it's a process, and one that you must invite God into every step of the way. When I decided to write this book one of the key pieces I wanted to include was a prayer to start every chapter. Why? Because God needs to be invited into this journey, each and every chapter.

God needs to be a part of our day, our growth, our faith walk, and when He is in control, AMAZING happens time and time again. Do not be discouraged if you start the forgiveness journal and do not feel automatically different, but at the same time, don't be surprised if you do. It will all depend on how open and transparent you with the process and inviting God to be a part of it. Each person is unique, there is no time frame, or gold star if you get through it faster or slower than the next.

This is about you and your foundation, building it per His instruction, and His timing. The beautiful part is that you are seeking Him, and you desire to strengthen your foundation of faith, or figure out how to get back to a place of faith! This process will begin with small incremental changes, from the inside, with God in control, fueling your Holy Spirit, transforming your heart, renewing your mind, creating a new you in Christ! It is a beautiful journey that you will never regret taking.

CHAPTER 3

Knowing Your Enemy

Father God,

Thank You for walking with me through this journey of faith. Father thank You for allowing me to reflect on areas of my own life that are broken, areas that I need to forgive myself for, and places I need to find forgiveness for others. Help me to recognize Your voice and grow in my discernment so I am not deceived by the enemy. Father allow these words to enrich my mind with wisdom, strength, and courage to grow stronger in my relationship with You.

In Jesus' Precious Name I Pray, Amen.

Satan is no one to fear. He is a master con-artist and deceiver, yes, but he loses the war. He is not on the same plane as God, he is not victorious. For a long time, I didn't know much about Satan. In fact, it was as if talking about the enemy was something you shouldn't do. Don't give power to his name, people would say.

Yet, any good defensive coach would tell you, you must study your opponent to understand how they play, in order to be prepared. Although you shouldn't fear the enemy, or give him more credit than what is due, it is imperative to know *how* he can attack you so that you can live in preparation, on guard, and when required, respond with a good offense to fight back!

Let's look at how we are warned that Satan will attack us. "Be sober-minded; be watchful. Your adversary the devil prowls around like a roaring lion, seeking someone to devour. Resist him, firm in your faith, knowing that the same kinds of suffering are being experienced by your brotherhood throughout the world" (1 Peter 5:8-9). This passage offers us guidance in a few areas of both awareness and humility.

First, is the instruction of being alert. Understanding that the enemy is literally prowling around like a lion who is hungry to eat, searching for prey. When a predator is looking for prey, they are pacing around, searching out prey that would be vulnerable, following packs from a distance, unseen and unheard. The enemy wants nothing more than for people to believe that he doesn't exist. Why? Because if you don't know about him, if you don't learn about how he works, then he can work in the background, unnoticed, and people will think it is everything else but him.

While he scowls around waiting to pick off the weakest one, or the one who wandered away or was least expectant, we are distracted by life and unprepared. God is saying to be aware for the enemy is real and seeking out believers to devour. The resistance we are given is both in our faith and our fellow believers.

"Firm in your faith" is a phrase that we see Paul speak about in Ephesians 6 when he talks about the Armor of God and resisting the enemy. The correlation between these two phrases spoken in Peter and then again in Paul is not coincidental. To stand firm in one's faith is a defense in and of itself against the prowling enemy. It is to be unmovable, unwavering, knowing the truth so well and planted so firmly in the foundation of Christ that schemes and attacks from the enemy fall ineffective to your progress.

Second, is to know that as followers of Christ we are all experiencing sufferings, trials, and attacks of various kinds from the enemy. We are not exempt from the negative struggles and occurrences that come with living in a fallen world. We are not exempt from the consequence of sin, even if we have been forgiven of it. We must know, that when we face these trials to not feel singled out, or alone, or that it is some sort of penance or recourse. Most importantly, do not abandon your faith in times of trails or pain. No, we are told here, stand firm, know that your brothers and sisters in Christ, all over the world are facing sufferings of the same kind. As we know today, from someone who lives in the comforts of the United States, our brothers and sisters in Christ in other parts of the world are facing persecution and trials that we cannot even fathom simply for believing in God, let alone the struggles that come with journeying through life itself.

We must stand firm with them, in our faith, in fervent prayer, and not be distracted by our first world issues that we forget there are real wars being waged against believers and there is a real battle occurring in the spiritual realm to keep people from following Christ and believing in God's goodness.

As I had said, in Ephesians 6, Paul tells us how to resist and fight the enemy, "Put on the whole armor of God, that you may be able to stand against the schemes of the devil. For we do not wrestle against flesh and blood, but against the rulers, against the authorities, against the cosmic powers over this present darkness, against the spiritual forces of evil in the heavenly places. Therefore, take up the whole armor of God, that you may be able to withstand in the evil day, and having done all, to stand firm" (Ephesians 6:11-16). There is that phrase again, to stand firm.

I want you for a moment, to envision yourself standing firm in the face of evil. I want you to see yourself standing firm, in the armor of God, as Satan prowls around you. You are aware of the enemy's presence, but you stand in the faith and foundation of victory in Jesus Christ. Therefore, the schemes of the enemy do not frighten you, or make you fearful. You stand boldly, as a soldier, fully armored, head held high, knowing you are protected with the fiercest protection and will be unmoved.

As Christians, we must not waver or sway when we face storms of this life, instead, we stand firm in our faith. For we do not wrestle against flesh and blood. We are fighting evil, and we must remember that with God on our side, we will always be victorious. We must remember to stand firm in His armor, to be aware of the enemy's deceptive ways, how he prowls around, and to be cognizant that we are not alone in our struggles or in our victory through Jesus Christ. We have an entire body of Christ, the church, that we can rely on for support, prayer, and to call on to go into battle, as we should be going into battle with them as well.

How many times have you thought you were fighting against a person, a situation, or even yourself? You have a major presentation to give that day, and the morning of you are arguing with your spouse, your kids are fighting all morning over the last bagel, you spilled coffee on your new blouse, hit several delays in traffic, and in your flesh, you want to scream! The enemy would be delighted if he could send you into this moment that you have been praying about completely distracted and distraught, angry, and all wound and bound up in your flesh.

If the enemy can get you out of the guidance of the Holy Spirit, if the enemy can get you so distracted that you react in your natural, then if you blow the presentation, you will walk away blaming God!

We all have done it. We all miss the connected domino effects of chaos to the enemy's attacks and fail to remember that we forgot to pause and pray. That is the enemy's hope, that he can slip in the background to be just a rough start to an important day, and keep you distracted enough that you didn't spend time with God, upset enough that you were operating from a place of flesh and not faith. That you don't see them as attacks because it was technically your husband, your kids fighting, backed up traffic, your clumsiness as you rushed to the car. He is the master of deception. A sequence of unfortunate events schemed ever so carefully to knock you completely out of faith and into your flesh. The Word, the truth that God has given us to understand the real battle that we will face in our journey through life is that the war is waged against a battle that cannot be seen with our eyes or fought with our hands.

What we are told is that we will face attacks from the enemy, from the spiritual realm of darkness, and we must not only be prepared, but resist them with the absolute truths of Christ. Priscilla Shirer says it best in her bible study book, Armor of God, which by the way I highly recommend to any and every one, "spiritual victory is directly connected to your ability to 'undisguise' the enemy. To uncover him. Unveil him. Unmask him. That's half the battle. But it's the half your enemy doesn't want you to pay much attention to, because once you do, you automatically begin to threaten his tyranny in your life."

One of the enemy's most vicious schemes against you is shaming you with your sin, your past, your previous mistakes. If you can understand that it is the enemy that is condemning you of a past that Jesus has already forgiven you for, and not God, then your battle is halfway won. In 2 Corinthians 2:11 Paul says, "In order that Satan might not outwit us. For we are not unaware of his schemes." If the enemy can keep us shackled in a place of feeling unworthy of God's mercy, if he can make us feel like a hypocrite if we step inside a sanctuary, if he can whisper these lies in our minds that we give attention to, we will continue to be distracted in defeat, instead of really accepting the One who can rescue us in our victory.

If we can understand that it is the enemy that we are battling, it is the enemy trying to keep us from God, it is not God who thinks these things of us, we can start putting power into prayer and defending ourselves against lies set out to stop us. It is not ourselves that we are fighting against, it is not a past we must try and earn forgiveness for, or an object that we are fighting, but a spiritual battle in a realm that we cannot see.

If we remember there is a real dark purpose in keeping us feeling guilty about the things that God has said there is mercy and grace, then we can turn our efforts away from fighting distractions and focus our energy toward rebuking Satan. Once you have achieved that understanding, your next step is accepting God's mercy and truly believing you are who He says you are in Christ Jesus.

I remember being faced with this battle just as I hung up the phone with my mom after she had told me to give it up to God. As I was desperately searching for a job, nearing that crossroad of homelessness, for the second time, and being forced to uproot my family and move us two hours back to my small hometown, I sat there in silence thinking about what she had said to me. You know, it all seemed very easy with my mom on the phone telling me to do so, I mean, I felt empowered at least. As soon as I was left to my own thoughts, my mind began to overflow with a storm of self-defeating blows.

Looking back now, I know it was the enemy. I know because I had been hiding from God for so long, the enemy knew this was an absolute necessary time to attack me. He had to do everything he could to keep me from returning to Christ and becoming anything powerful for the Kingdom of God.

The devil wanted my spirit to stay in turmoil, fear, worry, and sadness. Satan had to keep me from turning to the only One who could offer me a life full of peace, mercy, grace, joy, and a love that I had never before experienced.

Today, I am a walking testimony, everything about the way I live screams that I have something different, and I am consistently able to talk about my love and life with Jesus Christ. The enemy knows that a person who turns to God can be used by God. And so the prowling lion began to attack, and he filled my mind with the most condemning thoughts, reminding me of all the awful things I had done. He called me a hypocrite and flashed visions in my mind of me committing sins. My stomach began to churn.

I was reminded of my abortion, and this was the ultimate blow, and the one that had worked effortlessly before. In my mind, I could see those people screaming murderer, yelling that I was sentenced to hell. The pit in my stomach grew, the guilt and shame that flooded over me seemed as if it were truth. I could physically feel it.

Yet, the real truth was that I was so sorry and desperately wanted forgiveness. God had never left me, I had left him. The problem was, I didn't know the Word of God, I didn't know the absolute, unchanging truth. I didn't remember Scripture from my childhood, and I was too ashamed to talk to anyone who might know the truth.

If Satan can keep you from learning the Word, keep you too busy to open a Bible, try to convince you that you are too tired to go to church or Bible study, or that church is corrupt, then he can keep you from knowing the opposite of his lies.

Distracting you, scheming you, deceiving you away from God, from the church, from faith is one of his most deceptive and effective attacks he has. If you don't know the truth to combat his lies with, how much easier are his lies to sell to me, to you, and to anyone else he is trying to keep from God? When I speak about Satan's effectiveness in this type of deception, remember that this generation is now looking at one in four millennials that do not openly identify with faith at all. When you are at that place of being deceived away from the truth, it is easy to believe the lies. For me, I had no truth to combat those lies with, and at that point, I couldn't tell you anything about forgiveness either. I believed what those Christians screamed at me on the side of the road, because well, they were more Christian than I was.

Sixty percent of millennials believe that Christianity is judgmental. I can identify with this current faith crisis, and if they had experiences like mine, or have been exposed to a religious version via social media, I can understand their perception. As the body of Christ, we must do everything to change that perception by reflecting the truth of who Jesus Christ really is.

I thought because those who were screaming at me called themselves Christians they were telling me the truth. At least that is what I thought then. I don't think they knew that they had a major hand in the work of the enemy. What I saw out there on that road: judgment, hatefulness, anger; that wasn't Jesus.

I didn't know enough about Jesus to know that it wasn't Him that I was looking at in those people. I had no truth to combat the enemy with. The fact was, there was nothing that I could do to take those actions back in my past, and Satan knew that if he could keep me feeling horrible about them, feeling unworthy enough to turn to God, then I wouldn't. The enemy knew it had worked time and time again, so he kept doing it. If it ain't broke, why change it? The enemy is like mayhem from the Allstate commercial, a skilled ninja in making your life a living struggle. What is amazing is that the Word shows us exactly how to handle when the enemy attacks. We just have to make sure we are reading it and learning His truth so when the attacks happened, we are prepared enough to stand firm in our faith. Even Jesus Himself was tempted by the devil, yes, the Son of God was tried multiple times. So, don't think for a second that you or I are exempt from these attacks or attempts at deception or distraction.

Not only that, but we are shown that Satan waited until a time when Jesus was most vulnerable. Like the lion waiting for the weakest prey to fall out behind the pack or be distracted enough to not be prepared for his attack. Jesus had been in the wilderness, fasting for 40 days. I don't know about you, but I know the kind of mood I am in when I go without a meal or two, so I can only imagine the type of hunger and mental weariness that comes from a forty-day fast.

I am certain that the enemy, prowling around Jesus would have seen this as a weakness, and an opportune time to pounce. Look how Jesus handles that moment, "Then Jesus was led by the Spirit into the wilderness to be tempted there by the devil. For forty days and forty nights he fasted and became very hungry. During that time the devil came and said to him, 'If you are the Son of God, tell these stones to become loaves of bread.' But Jesus told him, 'No! It is written, 'People do not live by bread alone, but by every word that comes from the mouth of God.' Then the devil took him to the holy city, Jerusalem, to the highest point of the Temple, and said, 'If you are the Son of God, jump off! For it is written, 'He will order his angels to protect you. And they will hold you up with their hands, so you won't even hurt your foot on a stone.' Jesus responded, 'It is also written, 'You must not test the LORD your God.' Next the devil took him to the peak of a very high mountain and showed him all the kingdoms of the world and their glory. 'I will give it all to you,' he said, 'if you will kneel down and worship me.' 'Get out of here, Satan,' Jesus told him. 'For it is written, 'You must worship the LORD your God and serve only him.' Then the devil went away, and angels came and took care of Jesus" (Matthew 4:1-11).

We are shown here some pivotal keys in how the enemy attacks and how we are to respond. One, the enemy first attacked a core need that Jesus had, his hunger. Turn these stones to bread he told him. Now after 40 days of no food, I would really have thought long and hard about how I could turn those stones to loaves and feasted for days. That is why I am a work in progress and Jesus is the perfect Son of God who responded with the Word. Hebrews 4:12 says, "For the word of God is living and powerful, and sharper than any two-edged sword, piercing even to the division of soul and spirit, and of joints and marrow, and is a discerner of the thoughts and intents of the heart."

It is the Word of God that serves as our spiritual sword in combatting the enemy. In Ephesians 6 when Paul teaches us about the armor of God we are each given to combat in spiritual warfare, he says, "In addition to all this, take up the shield of faith, with which you can extinguish all the flaming arrows of the evil one. Take the helmet of salvation and the sword of the Spirit, which is the word of God." Notice that Paul references the fiery arrows of the evil one. Again, letting us know, Satan is going to try to attack you, that is his end game.

Jesus used the Word of God to combat the devil and we are instructed to do the same! It is not only in Scripture that we are told to do this, as we see in Ephesians, but we are shown its effective execution by Jesus Himself. If we continue to look at Jesus' battle with Satan in the wilderness we will see that the enemy didn't stop after his first attempt failed.

His second attack on Jesus was testing His faith and Satan quoted Scripture back to Jesus. Satan studies us, knows our moves, and uses uniquely crafted schemes to try and plot against us. Satan was twisting Scripture in a way to try and get Jesus to test the power of God. Wait, you mean Satan knows Scripture? You mean that sometimes I could be distracted by something that may look like it is almost the truth, but it could still be a scheme of the devil? Absolutely. Like the fact that your sin is truly something you committed. That is the truth. You did something that God has instructed you not to do, also the truth. The rest of the shame, guilt, condemnation that comes with it, after you ask for forgiveness in your heart, not truth. That is how the enemy's schemes are so tactful.

In fact, the Word specifically tells us that the devil doesn't come dressed up in a red leather jumpsuit, with horns, a pitchfork, and a tail shouting, "Will the real Lucipher please stand up? Hey y'all, I'm the devil." 2 Corinthians 11:14, "and no wonder for Satan himself masquerades as an angel of light." Yes, there will be times that Satan will attack you with something that appears to be almost truth or will be disguised as people who claim to follow Christ, but their teachings are not supported by the Word of God.

Jesus knew the truth, knew the Word and responded again with the Word of God. We have to be so rooted in our faith, that our decisions, actions, processes are in alignment with God's Word. That when we have something in question, we can compare it with the Word of God, for only then will we have discernment against an absolute, never changing truth. Even when Satan's second attempt failed, he tried a third time, tempting Jesus with power and glory. Jesus did not only respond with the Word of God but cast Satan away, and so the enemy had to flee. "Submit yourselves therefore to God. Resist the devil, and he will flee from you" (James 4:7).

You see, the enemy is going to attack you in a host of different ways and once you have become skilled in warding off his attacks in one area or by one means, he will try again utilizing something different. If he is going to try Jesus Himself, the Messiah, the Son of God, three separate times and Scripture said he left only to wait for a *more opportune* time to attack again, you can be certain that our walk will be riddled with attacks and schemes as well.

Our sin, our mistakes, our past, is one of the most influential ways the enemy attacks us because we know it was sin and there is nothing we can do to change it. We don't have the opportunity to say no and walk away, it is already done. The amazing part is that we have the power through Christ to completely remove this fiery arrow out of the arsenal the devil has to use against us.

That is right. We can completely eradicate that from his attack plan, because the beautiful part about an ugly past, is that God can be the only source of that transformation story. There is no condemnation in those who are in Christ Jesus, and that is the truth you run those feelings of guilt, shame, sadness, and anger by. When those feelings from your past mistakes don't align with the Word of God who tells you, 'My child you are forgiven and in Me there is no condemnation, there is no judgment', you let that go.

You must know your forgiveness in Christ, and your immeasurable worth in Him choosing you. Satan's sole purpose is to keep you from trusting God, to distract you from growing in your faith, from walking out your purpose, and spreading the good news about Jesus Christ.

If you feel unworthy, if you feel ashamed about what you have done, if you feel that you have messed up too bad for God, then the enemy will play on that repeatedly. It is a key way to keep you distracted from the truth, by making you live in fear or insecurity from the lies the enemy plants in your mind. It is not until you choose to believe the truth of Jesus Christ, the truth of His salvation, the truth about who you really are in Christ, that the enemy's attacks of condemnation on these areas of your past will no longer be effective.

"Behold, I have given you authority to tread upon serpents and scorpions, and over all the power of the enemy, and nothing shall injure you" (Luke 10:19). With that horrible pit in my stomach, I looked up to a God that I thought was really mad at me, really disappointed in me, and quite honestly, I thought wasn't going to care much at all about what I had to say, who knew I was only coming to Him now because of this mess th. I had created. I was truly the prodigal son just knocking on the door asking if I could be but a servant in the house somewhere.

Despite the lies the enemy kept shouting in my mind, sobbing on my knees, in the living room of my one-bedroom apartment, I lifted my hands to the ceiling and said, "God, I cannot do this on my own. I am so sorry for everything I have done. I know you are mad at me, all I can say is I am so sorry, please forgive me, God. I need you to help me. Take this, I can't do it anymore." I laid my face on the floor and cried this soul-cleansing cry.

As you read in the first chapter, this was part of my rescue. This was a major key to my testimony and who I am today in my faith. God answered, but it was bigger than just a couple of job interviews that turned into career opportunities. It was bigger than saving me from that hole I had dug myself into. I was the prodigal son, that finally came home, and God just opened His arms and said, my beautiful, worthy, daughter, I love you so much, welcome home.

CHAPTER 4

Renewing Your Mind

Father God,

    Thank You for loving me beyond my brokenness and being a place of refuge and restoration. In You, I can renew my thoughts about myself and find the truth in who I am. Allow me to take captive any thought that is not from You Lord, and rebuke it in the name of Your son Jesus Christ. Father allow me to grow in truly understanding and accepting who I am as a child of God, and the favor and blessing Your Kingdom inhabits. Thank You, Father, for loving me so much.

    In Jesus' Gracious Name I Pray, Amen.

In Chapter three I stressed how important it was to know the truth that God has given us in His Word. It is an essential part of responding to the attacks of Satan. However, knowing something and believing in what you know, are two very different things. To believe the truth in the Word one must have a mind that accepts it; Scripture talks about this acceptance of truth being a renewal of the mind. The renewal of one's mind occurs when you choose to align your thoughts, your actions, your processes in accordance with His Word. It is when you become aware of the enemy's attacks waging and yet you refuse to allow them to take root in your mental space, you refuse to allow seeds of darkness to be planted, let alone watered. It is choosing faith and then making a series of choices after to which support that choice of faith by what you do, what you think, what you say, and what you meditate on.

In Philippians 4:8, Paul instructs us to align our thoughts on that which is worthy of praise, "Finally, brothers and sisters, whatever is true, whatever is noble, whatever is right, whatever is pure, whatever is lovely, whatever is admirable--if anything is excellent or praiseworthy--think about such things." For many of us, this would be a total one-eighty to our thought life. To focus only on the positive, never entertaining negative thoughts, and believing in the Word of God, even when there is a storm raging around us. Having faith when it contradicts logic.

A transformation takes place once you choose to follow Christ, but there is also a discipline that facilitates that transformation that we can hold ourselves accountable to. I remember hearing about this at church quite a few times but not really understanding it. To be honest, I thought it was something much different than what it actually is. I mean in the Old Testament there were radical transformations, like Saul becoming Paul and living so obediently and passionately for God that it was literally a transformation like no other. A murderer of Christians to the author of most of the New Testament. Now that's a transformation!

I didn't realize that my own transformation was taking place, ever so gently in different ways, here and there. I remember talking to a friend about faith and she had no desire to come to Christ because, well she thought it was too boring to be a Christian. She didn't want to give up her more "exciting" lifestyle of the downtown nightlife and extracurricular activities that wouldn't necessarily be "faith-approved."

To be honest, when I first started going to church, there were a lot of things that I still did that were of the world. I still went out to the clubs, still drank too much alcohol from time to time, still cursed far too often, and a host of other things that should honestly, be expected of someone who was walking in fresh out of the world and into a life with Christ. As Christians, we need to do a better job of having grace and an expectation that everyone is a work in progress, and we all come to Christ at different points, with different levels of broken, and different areas of growth to begin working on.

Some of us are coming into God's house as the prodigal son, the lost sheep, and God wants us all to be rejoicing, celebrating, welcoming our new follower into the body of Christ. We should encourage and embrace one another out of our mutual love for Jesus Christ. As that love for Christ grows, the internal transformation begins. The Holy Spirit takes root and begins working in ways that we aren't even fully aware of. Christ Himself wasn't looking for me to be anything other than myself, if I tried to fix my broke *before* coming to Church, I would have never stepped foot inside His house.

He's going to do the changing with me and He doesn't want it if we don't choose it with a heart that desires it. "Therefore, if anyone *is* in Christ, *he is* a new creation; old things have passed away; behold, all things have become new" (2 Corinthians 5:17). When I first started following Christ I didn't really feel new or different, I was just interested, I felt lucky that God hadn't given up on me. I just knew I had a lot of work to do.

Some days I felt overwhelmed at how much work needed to be done! God ever so gently would speak to me, yes speak to me, and simply say, one step at a time, I am not seeking perfection, only progress. What a relief! I would continually tell others around me, I am a work in progress who loves her some Jesus.

At first, I think I was saying this because I felt like such a mess, I just wanted people to know out loud that I knew I wasn't where I felt everyone else was. So, I was as open as I could be, so that they knew that I knew, I needed God to work on me and that was why I was here. What I realized so quickly was that the more open I was with people about my brokenness, the bolder I became about my walk and what God was working on with me, the more open others became in sharing their struggles, their broken, and their transformation stories. I suddenly realized I was surrounded by broken people! Amazingly, beautiful, broken people who were in love with Jesus.

So, I continued to seek God, to be a little bit better than who I was the day before. I included Him in my prayer life, attended all the church that I could. The more I could learn, the more I could apply, or at least attempt to. I still struggled along the way, but little by little the things that used to appeal to me no longer did. I was making choices that were supporting my faith, watering the renewal of my mind, and allowing the transformation to take root. I remember one day hearing someone use the Lord's name in vain and it pierced my ears like no other! I was honestly shocked. Not that they used His name in vain, I was shocked that it hurt me so! When did that happen? That is when I really started becoming aware of my own transformation. Others took notice as well, making comments about my joy, light, and conversation. How much different I seemed to be then a year ago, or when they had met me. I would simply give glory to God and thank Him for being patient with my hot mess work in progress.

"You were taught, with regard to your former way of life, to put off your old self, which is being corrupted by its deceitful desires; to be made new in the attitude of your minds; and to put on the new self, created to be like God in true righteousness and holiness" (Ephesians 4:21-23). That is what was happening without me even being aware, my old self was being put away, as if it were last season's wardrobe and article by article God was boxing it up and replacing it with something brand new. A new attitude of the mind, a new self, to be created like God in true righteousness and holiness. How amazing is that!

There is nothing about your old self God sees when you chose to give your heart to Him. You may still struggle with it, but that is because you are going back to the Cross and picking things up that Jesus already died for. These powerful verses in addition to the one at the beginning of this chapter, Romans 12:2, read clear in teaching us that we *are* made new in Christ, becoming more like Him as we grow in our faith. What is amazing is that all I had to do was seek God and He took care of the transforming.

The more I fed my spirit, the more I fell in love with who Jesus is, the more God transformed my heart, which changed my mind, which shaped my actions and words. It's amazing and incredible! I get more excited to attend Praise and Worship Night than I ever did for a night out downtown at the clubs! And God did all of that, all I had to do was seek Him! Who I desire in a spouse has changed drastically, from seeking attributes of the world, to prioritizing values of faith and a man of God. I have become a better parent in ways that bring tears to my eyes because my kids deserve the best mom in the entire world, and God has given me the ability to have these amazing, impactful conversations, and He is helping me raise them to be these awesome humans. My actions, values, and choices have become more aligned with my walk. Trust me I still struggle, I will always be a work in progress, but I am amazed at what God has done in my life.

One of the most important ways to grow in our faith and renew our minds is to replace worldly logic with the truth of Jesus. And that is found solely in God's living Word! I went through a season during my walk when I only wanted to study what Jesus said and taught while He was on earth. If I wanted to grow in my faith, who better to learn from? I loved reading and re-reading the Gospels, it was if every time I read a verse I would get a new revelation in my spirit.

The way Jesus taught was incredible and allowed me to respect His way of teaching in addition to what He had to say. If you knew that you were sent into the world to die for the forgiveness of sins, forgiveness would probably be a lesson you would make sure people understood, right?

I mean, in Luke 15 Jesus used three different ways to describe how you are accepted even after you are lost. You see, renewing your mind is a key part to removing power from your past and in order to remove power from your past is to learn that you don't live there anymore. To understand this, we will look at Jesus teaching about forgiveness in the Gospel of Luke 7:36-50.

In this Chapter, Jesus is going to dinner at a Pharisee's house, and as he is standing there a woman who is known in town as a sinner came to where Jesus was. She stood behind Him, wept at His feet covering them with tears, and anointed His feet with perfume. The Pharisee questioned the authenticity of Jesus as a prophet, saying if He were, He would know this woman was a sinner and would not let her keep company near Him. Jesus responded with a parable regarding debts, one who owed a little, and one who owed a great deal, though neither could repay, and so both debts were forgiven in full. He asked, which person would love the person who forgave those debts more, the one with little debt or the one with a lot of debt. The Pharisee responded, the one with the most debt. Jesus responds with a statement regarding those who have been forgiven the most, love in return the most, and turns to the woman, forgives her of her sins, and says to her, "your faith has saved you, go in peace."

There have been many times that I have uttered the phrase as if dying on the Cross for me wasn't enough, Jesus had to rescue me from myself in present time, for me to feel forever indebted to Him. I relate to the woman crying at His feet and find amazing peace and mercy in Jesus' words. That is His truth, and any time you doubt if His forgiveness covers you, if it is real, if it was really meant for you, or for that time, or that mess up, the answer is always yes. A hundred times, Jesus says yes, because He chose you, when He saw it all, felt it all, hanging, crucified on that Cross, He chose you. And yes, you are truly forgiven.

When doubt creeps in, when the enemy casts question into your mind, you respond with the truth of Jesus. I am covered by the blood of Jesus Christ, forgiven, righteous and redeemed. My faith has saved me. That statement will shut the enemy down and the feelings of guilt, condemnation, and shame will disappear. The enemy cannot withstand the truth and word of Jesus Christ. When you fight back with His word, you will be victorious, every single time. This will begin to build your confidence in showing you those condemning feelings are not of God, but the one who wants to keep you from Him.

This action of shutting down the lies and replacing it with God's truth, rebuking Satan in the name of Jesus is the discipline of faith that I spoke of earlier in this Chapter. You must re-train your thought process to not allow those lies to settle in. Sometimes we can be so used to hearing those lies, to believing what the world says, what that enemy has planted, that we become comfortable in accepting it. We allow those thoughts to run a course of darkness in our thought process. We give them time, energy, emotion, and power in our lives.

Utilizing discipline would be knowing immediately when you begin to think those negative thoughts—those thoughts or feelings that are not praiseworthy and bring you fear or shame, guilt or angst—immediately shut them down with prayer, and I mean immediately. Rebuke them in the name of Jesus Christ because you are a righteous child of God that is redeemed, loved, and worthy. Pray to God for protection over your mind, your thoughts, and your emotions. Ask Him to help you renew your mind to be aligned with His truth of who you are and the freedom you have in Him. That is being obedient to His word and staying disciplined in your faith. Not watering those thoughts will shut them down and allow you to water the truth we are given in Philippians 4:8.

You may think it sounds ridiculous, but just as I said with the forgiveness journal, there are things that you are going to have to put into practice and make yourself do before they become a part of who you actually are. A negative thought doesn't have to spiral out of control into worry and stress and anxiety unless you choose to give it time in your mind to fester. Shut it down, respond with a truth and promise from God, and keep it moving.

Once you can forgive yourself, and accept the forgiveness that Christ has for you, the enemy has no power in your past. Satan cannot condemn you effectively if you know there is no condemnation in Christ. If you begin to really grasp a hold of these truths, living in forgiveness, and walking the path to forgiving yourself and embracing Christ's forgiveness for you, the power that used to lie in your past is gone. You are renewing the way you think, grasping the mindset of the child of God that you are, disciplining yourself to live in that truth, and being bold enough to bask in your weakness because that is where His power and glory lies!

Qualifications in Christ

Feeling like we are forgiven from our past and understanding how we can be useful to God can sometimes come with a series of questions… What would God want with someone like me? With all of my mess, and my brokenness, how could I possibly be of any use to God? These questions of self-doubt in regard to fulfilling God's purpose is all a part of this transformation process.

If you still view yourself as a reflection of your past, or in the eyes of the world, you will not see the strength and power God has in store for you. In fact, understanding the possibility of your effectiveness with God will shed light on why the enemy wants to keep you from God, or keep you ineffective in carrying out His purpose.

If you browse through the Bible you will find a host of "unqualified" people that Jesus called to fulfill the purpose of the Kingdom. Even Moses tried to convince God he wasn't the man for the job when God called him to lead the Israelites to the Promised Land. We focus on how he parted the Red Sea, jotted down the commandments for all of mankind, and spoke directly with God. Those are true and powerful pieces of Moses' walk but what people skip over is that Moses' also struggled to see his own qualifications in being useful to God's calling.

"But Moses said to God, "Who am I that I should go to Pharaoh and bring the Israelites out of Egypt?" (Exodus 3:12). Moses felt unworthy to fulfill this mission, asking God Himself, but who I am to do this? If he would've listened to his own thoughts instead of the truth that God tells him in Exodus 3:13, saying to Moses, "certainly I will be with you and this will be a sign to you that I sent you…" it would have kept him from fulfilling God's purpose and some major plans for the Israelites!

There are so many people in the Bible that if left to the standards of the world, or even the Pharisees for that matter, would have been shut out, counted out, and considered useless to God's mission. Remember that God used all types of people throughout Scripture to fulfill His purpose and expand His Kingdom. Jacob was a cheater, Peter had denied Christ, Noah was a drunk, Jonah ran from God, Sara was impatient, David had an affair, Rahab was a prostitute, Joseph was abused, and Lazarus was dead!

God tells us in 2 Corinthians 12:9, "My grace is sufficient for you for my power is made perfect in weakness." You see, Jesus doesn't call the qualified, He qualifies the called. God uses the messes we were so ashamed of to become messages we can stand on, and minister from, so others can be uplifted in faith while they are walking through the same kind of mess.

Romans 8:28 says, "And we know that in all things God works for the good of those who love him, who have been called according to his purpose." God can use anything and turn it into something good. He can use your mess to bless because God is the One who turns the test into a testimony. To really understand the depth of this truth, one must read the stories of the various people the world would have counted out, but God called righteous, worthy, and more than useful for the Kingdom!

Earlier, I spoke about one of the most radical transformations found in the Old Testament. This story is in Acts chapter 9: along Damascus Road when Saul is converted. Saul had been crucifying those who followed Jesus Christ, murdering them, seeking out their names to hunt them down. This is what he was known for, he was feared by believers.

Now, I know I have some stuff in my past, and I also know that sin isn't weighted on some scale to God, sin is sin. But can you imagine being the guy that had gone around killing Christians? That was your claim to fame? Talk about some mess!

Well that was Saul's path, his boasted broken, until God Himself spoke to Him from a light in the heavens, and Saul dropped to his knees, trembling, knowing it was the Lord God who was speaking to Him. Saul was blinded by that light for three days and given specific orders of which he followed. His sight was returned through the prayer and touch of Ananias, who mind you was not too excited that he was the chosen one to go and touch the Christian killer but did so as an act of faith.

When Ananias touched Saul, the Bible said his sight returned as if scales fell off from his eyes. Like scales falling, or shedding, this to me is symbolic of Saul's transformation. It didn't say that Saul's sight was returned, but like scales falling from his eyes, his sight was returned. He had shed his blindness, and now he could see.

Saul then arose and was baptized. He began preaching the message of Jesus, escaping the very persecution he himself used to terrorize others with, and his strength and faith grew. He even began using the Latin form of his name, Paul, which was more familiar to the Gentiles to which he was preaching the message, unlike Saul which was of the Pharisee past he had lived. See, even this slight variation of a name change, you can see how God was renewing Paul's mind.

Paul considered who would hear his message of Christ., Thus, he was no longer Saul of the Hebrew language, the Pharisee man, a religious icon, who persecuted Christians. He was Paul, of the Latin origin, a follower of Christ, sharing the message of the Son of God to the Gentiles. His mind renewed, as was his heart, his message, his life, and in this instance, even his name.

Apostle Paul is known as the most prolific writer in all the Bible and in fact, of the twenty-seven books in the New Testament, Paul was originally ascribed to thirteen of them. Scholars agree on the following eight books: Galatians (AD 47), 1 Thessalonians (AD 51), 1 and 2 Corinthians and Romans (AD 52-56), Colossians, Philippians, and Philemon (AD 60-62); and whether Paul was the actual author, or if it was transcribed later from Paul's perspective, is debated on the following five: 2 Thessalonians (AD 51-52), Ephesians (AD 60-62), 1 Timothy and Titus (AD 62), 2 Timothy (AD 63-64).

Now mind you, the books of the Bible went through some vigorous review to be determined canon and ensured they were inspired by God, the Holy Spirit, historically accurate, etc. So, you can be confident that God indeed chose to use a man who was a murderer, yes even of Christians, post-transformation, to fulfill His will for the Kingdom.

It was Saul's choice to repent in his heart, fall to his face with remorse, and fear of the Lord. It was his choice to be baptized and give his life to God. Saul chose to follow God despite his murderous past and God used Saul to become a powerful message to believers despite the mess he was delivered from. It could have easily stopped there, and salvation and forgiveness were Saul's.

Yet, in the process of learning about God, accepting His forgiveness and grace, building a relationship, Paul became so consumed with the Spirit that he began serving Him each day thereafter.

Paul could have easily let his past torment him, keeping him shackled and useless, but instead, he became a living testimony glorifying a powerful, transformative God. He nailed his sins to the Cross and moved forward, a new person in Christ!

God offers each of us that same renewal and transformation too. He is the same then as He is now, and always will be! Jesus knew you were worth dying for. He saw the same in Saul and made sure to include the very details of Paul's transformation story and inspired Him to write so much of the New Testament to then inspire us. There is an overarching message of mercy and grace in the transformation of Saul to Paul that God designed. When Jesus looks at you, He sees a child of God that was worth His death on the Cross. If you don't see yourself as being of value, what worth does that place on His sacrifice?

The moment you doubt your worth to God, or the enemy tries to remind you of your past, you have all of the tools and truth to remove the power from it. You are not defined by the choices you made or the past you had; you don't live there anymore!

The moment you chose to follow Christ, you became new in Christ, a new creation, and your transformation began. That doesn't mean instantaneous! It means you are a work in progress with God working through the Holy Spirit on the inside of you, creating a new you! (2 Corinthians 5:17). The hard part is believing that Scripture is as true for you, as it was for Paul and the many other people in the Bible whom God has transformed.

The truth is, this book isn't just for Christians struggling to dive deeper in their faith, or people who have yet to begin their walk. This is also for Christians who have forgotten what it means to follow Jesus Christ and reflect the King. It is for Christians who have become too caught up in religion that self-righteousness replaces His righteousness, and on the journey to knowing Him, they become comfortable in telling others what He is not. Wherever you are in your walk, you have the tools and truth to become a more powerful, effective follower of Jesus Christ!

As the body of Christ, we have a perspective shift that we much initiate in the world today. Somehow, the message of Jesus' love, mercy, and grace has gotten lost in religious law. As we walk this out together, I know we can start becoming more impactful Christians and thus a more genuine body of Christ.

CHAPTER 5

Finding Your Freedom in Christ

Father God,

Thank You for creating me with a specific purpose and for gifting me with abilities that are unique to my plan. Thank You for seeing me as who I am meant to be, through the fulfillment of Your plan, not just who I am today. Father allow me to fulfill myself in You, with You. Help me to break every bond that is holding me back from walking in true freedom with You.

In Jesus' Powerful Name I Pray, Amen.

The enemy reminded me of every awful thing I had done since I was like seven, yes, there were things upon things. I am telling you, Satan is great at scheming and plotting this weaved wonder of horrible distraction that can knock you off your path when you least expect it.

He shamed and mocked my life so much, that guilt kept me from stepping foot inside of a church. Each time he would succeed at keeping me away from God's presence, or God's Word for a few more months, then the months turned to years, and the next thing I know I was talking to someone about how it had been eight years since I had walked into a sanctuary. Really, eight years?

Then I would feel ashamed about how long I had been away from Church, and the enemy would add that to the list of wrongs and twist it into some deceitful lie about how the building would burst into flames when I walked in. Sound familiar?

Until we remove that power from our past, the enemy can always use it to drive a wedge between us and God. I've talked about how he can shame you with it, how you can respond when that happens, the grace that God offers to you if you accept it, and how worthy you are to accept that mercy. What about the actual past that you are carrying? You know, that luggage we can't seem to shake; the mistakes, scars, hurt, and betrayals? We take it from relationship to relationship, or keep it buried somewhere deep down inside. It's those chains you often hear about. So, what if you are still struggling with the *stuff* itself?

For me, when it came to *my* past, and *my* chains, I seriously felt I was the exception to grace. There had to be fine print somewhere, in the caves, on a dead sea scroll perhaps, that someone missed. I was certain that I could simply not be forgiven. I mean, we're talking about a decade of bad decisions here, plus the big one that I knew I was damned for...

Any time I tried to actually think about those things with any sort of detail or focus, I would get overwhelmed feeling like it was all too much; I had exceeded God's grace quota. I could imagine God's mercy and grace for others and think about how wonderful and beautiful that is. For me though, well, let's just say this was prior to me understanding the depths of Paul's mercy and Peter's guilt, yet God proved unyielding grace for them both. I just couldn't face own stuff.

Now, I've talked about God giving us story after story of "hot messes," people who were murderers, adulterers, liars, thieves, and cheaters. God shows up people that were full of mess and sin, and He not only forgave them but transformed them and used them for amazing purposes. I talked about the amazing transformation story of Saul to Paul and how incredibly impactful that is for believers still today.

I say all of that to pose this question, don't you think there is another reason those stories are shared throughout Scripture? A purposeful reason that God tells us what those specific sins were? God didn't say, Paul did some things that we won't talk about, no, Paul *murdered* Christians. Scripture doesn't state, Peter said some things that were hurtful, no, Peter denied Jesus Christ three times!

God tells us the depths of these sins, so we can see that there is nothing too great that the blood of Jesus Christ cannot wash clean! You see, your sin, your mistakes, your failures and weaknesses aren't a disappointment to God. What I mean by that is He knows your beginning from your end.

To be disappointed is to have an expectation unrealized. It is not possible for God to have an expectation if He already knows. Therefore, you have not disappointed Him, He saw it all and sent His Son to die for you anyway. Choosing to carry that shame and guilt or walk with unforgiveness with you is saying that what Jesus did on the cross wasn't good enough.

I am revisiting this point one more time because before we start getting into the freedom of Christ. If you are not forgiving yourself for some of the things you have done in your past, then look at these examples and gain some perspective knowing that God did not forgive them on a contractual basis. Forgiveness was not earned by them, it was given prior to their good works.

I am forgiven. I know this because the condemnation I used to think was God, it used to terrify me from talking about my past. Once I walked out every chapter of this book, I am now living free in Christ! Free enough to share my transformation story absent shame or guilt, glorifying His name as the author.

I know it is hard to say the word abortion out loud. I know it is hard to talk about things we are disappointed in ourselves for, or that we wish we could change. The glory is not in what we have done, the glory is in what Jesus did and what God is able to do. God has mercy for us, and because of this we are transformed, renewed, saved people! It isn't easy to speak about divorce, adultery, molestation, alcoholism, drug abuse, rape, and a host of other sin or tough situations that our past can be made up of.

Until you can talk about, and I don't mean glorify, but talk about it, and glorify God who has delivered you from it, you will be chained to it. Like I said, for some of us our mess, will later become a message God wants us to use for someone else walking through a similar situation. If we are too paralyzed with guilt or too ashamed to be open, the enemy has the power over us and we could be missing out on opportunities to share our testimony and give glory to God.

The wiser I become, or a better way of saying it is *"the older I get,"* the more I have learned to appreciate that the greatest things in life are the ones that take work, risk, sacrifice, and are sometimes scary. In the end, those are the things that have proven time and time again to offer the greatest reward. Our faith is not grown in comfortable places! The most beautiful part about my ugly mess is that it now offers a beginning to my amazing transformation; I am a walking testimony to the love, mercy, and grace of Jesus Christ.

You see, if I fail to acknowledge the girl who was lost in the world seeking to fill voids with alcohol, drugs, and bad relationships. If I don't mention the woman who spent time homeless, wondering how life was going to work out for her and her two kids, = angry and scared. If I am too afraid of judgment to acknowledge that was my past, how can I give glory to God for transforming me to my present? The most amazing part of this is that the more I boast in my weakness and glorify God for His grace and mercy, the less useful it becomes to the enemy and at the same time people who are broken are becoming more confident to talk about their broken.

Satan cannot torment me or anyone else with a past used as a testimony to glorify our King! Do you see that the very thing the enemy used to terrify me with, that kept me afraid of turning to God, is now the entire first chapter of this very book? What the enemy intended for harm, God certainly used for good! A transformation that only can be found in the freedom of living in Christ. Being vulnerable is scary and our sins may be different, but every Christian has a past and we need to start becoming more comfortable and bold with that being a part of our story and not judging others when they are at their beginning or their testimony has yet to begin. If Jesus Himself were to say today as He did back then, "*let he without sin cast the first stone*," not a single soul could even pick up a shadow of a pebble. It's the beautiful part of grace, and the connection we must all acknowledge in our walk together.

The enemy loves to prey on our past because life doesn't offer a rewind button, it doesn't come with an eraser, and there are no do-overs. Many of us think back on our past sin and become really discouraged in our walk with God or feel hypocritical when trying to talk to others about their own walk. It can obstruct our growth in Christ or create a detour from our purpose if we are afraid to talk with Him. If the enemy can make us doubt our worth or validity in Christ, we become ineffective Christians, and that is a win for the enemy because you aren't doing anything for the Kingdom.

For years it's as if I was hiding from Christ, thinking to myself that eventually when I got myself together, then I would go back to Him. Somehow, the more I tried to do life without Christ, the deeper the hole, the heavier the burden, and the thicker the shame that weighed on my heart. My mind became a playground for the enemy, allowing me to think what I was feeling was truth, instead of answering with the Word of God.

What I know *now* is that the transformation occurs *with* Christ, not before, and the place I am inviting you to in this chapter is a place of real freedom through that transformation process. I didn't know turning to God was going to transform me into a woman I never knew I could be. I didn't know that turning to God was going to allow me to see in myself things I never knew I was capable of.

I turned to God because I was barely surviving and couldn't do life the way I was living it anymore, but God responded in His amazing way. God wants you in your broken, in your mess, for in that He says, "My grace is sufficient for you, for my power is made perfect in weakness" (2 Corinthians 12:9). Literally, we are told that in our weakness, in our mess, God's grace is enough. His power transforms, His strength delivered, and His grace more than enough for whatever mess we find ourselves in. The key is allowing Him into it!

Even after I started attending church I was afraid to talk to others about the past I had lived. I was terrified they would judge me, or not want me to be a part of their congregation. I was afraid if they knew the things I had done it would somehow change the love I had in my heart for Jesus. When it came to those outside the church, the enemy plagued my mind with self-defeating thoughts in hopes to keep me quiet about my love for Christ. Satan seared my mind with images of who I used to be, reminding me of the burdens of my past.,. Who am I to talk about Jesus with all the parties I have been to and worldly things I had done? Hypocrite. These fallacies kept me quiet, in fear, and in shame for far too long. There are many believers, some of you reading this right now that are currently in the very same place I was. Well, it is time to shed the scales from your eyes.

Freedom in Christ

Imagine if I never opened up about my broken? What if I had kept it shackled away somewhere down inside, afraid of who might find out, afraid of being judged, afraid that if people knew my mess, my validity as a person or as a Christian would somehow hold less weight? What if I never became bold enough in my faith or in my transformation?

There was a time when my past would paralyze me. The simple thought of my sin, talking about it, thinking about it, the reminder of what I knew but kept hidden left me bonded in a way you cannot fully understand until you have broken free from it. It's that pit in your stomach as a kid when you've done something wrong, so each time your mom says your name your stomach drops to your toes because you think you've been had. It is fear. The phrase the truth shall set you free is so much more powerful than we give it credit. Let me explain.

Freedom in Christ is a hard concept to grasp when looking through the lens of religion or as many define it—legalism. Religion often talks about works: what you should do, shouldn't do, and in our logic that is a total contradiction to our view of freedom. I mean, when I think about freedom I see myself, arms wide, standing in the sun, in a meadow somewhere, with no one around to tell me what to do. There's no ticking clock reminding me of deadlines or schedules, just me, the sun, and miles of space. No, I am not auditioning for the Sound of Music anytime soon but that thought alone allows me to take one of those big deep relief-in-exhale breaths.

Legalism is more about following rules and works to garnish salvation and leaves you with a feeling that following Christ is a laundry list of things to do and not to do. It sounds more like a Monday at work than a relationship with Jesus. Our salvation was deemed complete—finished when Jesus Christ sacrificed Himself on the cross in Calvary. We struggle with this because we have been conditioned in the world to believe that everything worth having must be *earned*. That nothing in life is free. Therefore, this idea of salvation without works, or a God who loves us because we are His creation, a forgiveness that doesn't require penance, but only a heart that truly desires reconciliation, innately conflicts with what we have been conditioned to believe.

When Jesus gave His Sermon on the Mount to a group of believers, we find Him teaching in a way that challenges what believers thought and replacing that with truth, His truth. In Matthew 5, Jesus continuously repeats this phrase, "You have heard that it was said… But I say to you…" He is replacing what believers thought they knew through religion with His truth as the Son of God. The same goes for us today, we must unlearn what we have been conditioned to believe by the world, in order to fully grasp the foundation of our faith as followers of Jesus and enter into a real relationship with Christ. Wait, what? I have to unlearn to learn? This may sound confusing, but it really isn't.

For the purpose of this process, forget everything that religion has taught you. Forget everything the world has said about Christians, everything you think you know based on watching other Christians and just focus on Jesus. Your end goal should be to build a relationship with *Him* and to understand who *He* really is, and who *you* are in *Christ*. So, what does that mean?

We can start with understanding who we are Christ Jesus. The moment you confessed, (and if you haven't yet, I hope you will by the end of this chapter, or book), that you believe Christ died for your sins, resurrected into heaven, and you choose to follow Him with all your heart and make Him your Lord and Savior, is the moment that you became someone different. You became a new creation, right then and there.

In the last chapter, we talked about the renewal or transformation of our mind, but there is so much more that Christ tells us we are when we declare Jesus Christ our Savior and King. Understanding who God says you are is a huge part of transforming your mind from the worldly view of who you were and stepping into the person that God now sees.

Scripture is filled with truths about who we are in Christ. Believing that you are these things is a journey in and of itself. Reading these truths, and knowing they exist, are crucial for responding to attacks from the enemy as you move closer to freedom and begin breaking the bondage of your past.

In reading Colossians, Ephesians, Philippians, Corinthians, Romans, and the Gospels one can find most of the 50 plus scriptures that speak directly to who you are in receiving Christ as your Lord and Savior. "You are complete in Him, which is the head of all principality and power" (Colossians 2:10); "You are holy and blameless before Him in love" (Ephesians 1:4); "I have no lack for my God supplies all of my need according to His riches in glory by Christ Jesus" (Philippians 4:19); "I am more than a conqueror through Him who loves me" (Romans 8:37); "I am an ambassador for Christ" (2 Corinthians 5:20); "I am forgiven of all my sins and washed in the blood" (Ephesians 1:7); "I am delivered from the power of darkness and translated into God's kingdom" (Colossians 1:13); and "I am redeemed: and free in Christ" (Galatians 3:13).

These truths and the many more that I did not reference but can be found in the books listed state the facts about who you are in Christ. These words are powerful, and it is imperative for our growth in Him that we try to understand and more importantly make every effort to fully accept these truths as our new identity in Christ. God is in the transformation business and has been since He began, but He will not force the transformation on you.

Free will is bigger than just the choice to believe in Christ. It involves every choice along our journey, growing in Him is a choice, offering forgiveness to others is a choice, following His guidance and instruction in the Word is a choice. Just as Saul chose every choice by free will after gaining back his sight to follow Christ: changing his name to Paul and becoming one of the most powerful deliverers of the New Testament. You and I have choices every day as to how we spend our time, how we respond to people, if we pause and pray before reacting, if we rebuke that negative thought, and so on.

As with any choice, you must first understand what you are choosing between. Salvation is all about what Jesus did for us, while who we become in Him is based on what we ourselves allow Jesus to do within us. Acceptance of the truth, growth in our relationship with Christ, and the walk that we embark on with our faith all are determined by consistent choices. You can read the words, "I am forgiven of all my sins and washed in the blood," but if you don't choose to believe that, you will continue to carry around baggage and burdens that Jesus already took for you at the cross. We can't thank God sacrificing His Son and then carry around shame and guilt for sin asked to be forgiven of. You are contradicting the power of the Cross, either what Jesus did was enough, or it wasn't? What you have done is not who you are, and God promises us that His grace is enough!

Some may be read this to gain perspective in order to help others with their past because theirs is not that difficult. That is great, we all walk a different road. The journey to claim our identity in Christ doesn't have to be plagued with a negative past. Even after I was able to fully accept the grace of God in dealing with my past mess, it's as if I was counteracting it with things of this world. Sometimes our identity as believers, regardless of your past, needs to go through a faith-check. Run it by the Word to see if you are holding yourself accountable to the truth you are called to live by.

There have been numerous times throughout my life that I have been asked to provide a biography, sometimes short other times long. Yet, each one asks me to provide a description to an audience that would qualify me as an expert on the subject matter to which I am presenting. Thus, each bio is slightly tailored to the experience, skill set, education, and accolades that support the topic at hand. When you think about it, we are constantly giving a biography of ourselves throughout life. In interviews, on dates, when one asks us the age-old question, "so tell me a little bit about yourself," we then unfold our personal biography.

As a woman, identity is something very important to me, mainly because I think it can be one of our biggest battles. We look in the mirror and we see everything that is wrong, every flaw, every scar, every dimple and not so fine line that is in the wrong place, and that all forms our identity. So many worldly influences constantly telling us what is wrong, we are on a constant hunt for identifiers to balance ourselves out. So, many of my triumphs, such as earning multiple degrees, becoming civically engaged and politically active, advancing in my career, became pieces of my identity that I was very proud of. Raising two children on my own, balancing their life, plus my career, activities, faith, and managing this very well, I was proud of this. Therefore, the label "independent mother of two," became a new piece to my identity that I wore with considerable pride.

However, one Tuesday as I sat in my women's bible study we spoke of our identity. We were asked to think of how we identified ourselves as women, and then how we identified ourselves as women of God. Did these identifiers match? I started to think of the many biographies I had written in the past, always starting with the degrees I had earned, moving then to the titles of the positions I had held, or the single mother status I so proudly wore. Although these were all things I had accomplished, I realized I carried pride in labels, that in fact, my biography in itself was one of self-pride, worldly accomplishment, and as far as a woman of God, He may get a sentence or two in reference to "active in her church community."

Then it hit me, a moment of beautiful conviction. I had never realized that these things I had been so incredibly proud of, were great achievements, but had nothing to do with *who* I was, *who* I am, and *who* I am becoming. My identity cannot be found in what I have accomplished, those are just things, and my identity is not some string of labels created by the world to make it easier to understand what box to check on an application, or to determine what tax credit I qualify for. I am a daughter of the King! I am an heir of the Most High! Scripture tells me what that means I am, and it is far better than anything I have ever put down in a biography to try and prove that I am worthy to give a presentation or write an article.

So, now if I ask you, who are you, what is your identity, what would you say? I want you to remove the labels of the world, because although you may fulfill roles, a mother, a husband, a professional, a friend, that is not who you *are*. Again, we look to these very defining Scriptures of who God tells us we are in Him: You are chosen, holy, and, blameless.

"For he chose us in Christ before the foundation of the world that we may be holy and unblemished in his sight in love" (Ephesians 1:4). You are redeemed and forgiven by the grace of Christ. "In Him we have redemption through His blood, the forgiveness of our trespasses, according to the riches of His grace" (Ephesians 1:7). Your new self is righteous and holy. "Put on the new man who has been created in God's image—in righteousness and holiness that comes from truth" (Ephesians 4:24). You have wisdom, righteousness, sanctification, and redemption. "He is the reason you have a relationship with Christ Jesus, who became for us wisdom, from God and righteousness, and sanctification and wisdom" (1 Corinthians 1:30). You have been sealed with the Holy Spirit of promise. "And when you heard the word of truth, when you believed in Christ, you were marked with the seal of the promised Holy Spirit" (Ephesians 1:30).

Redefining Yourself

When someone asks you who you are, the words that should run through your mind are free, loved, favored, redeemed, righteous, holy, wise, promised, blameless, sanctified, an heir to the King. To the world we would sound crazy, we would sound so different, and odd! They may dislike you and judge you if you say something like that. Yet Jesus says, "If you belonged to the world, it would love you as its own. As it is, you do not belong to the world, but I have chosen you out of the world. That is why the world hates you" (John 15:19). And although the world may not hate you because of a biography that talks of being holy, loved, and redeemed, God tells us that we will be viewed as different, disliked, and possibly hated for following Jesus.

Who you are in Christ, those defining characteristics were defined by the One who created us. Those are things we cannot question! He created you, He knows who you are meant to be, what you are capable of! When I surrendered to God, I had no idea He would be transforming me into the woman of God I am today. I had no idea that I would be capable of the things I am today. God knew. You are a child of God and before and after everything else that is the core of who you truly are. He has given us amazingly different gifts, and our inner self does not lessen those at all.

What I want you to define is the depth of who you are as a child of the King. You are not defined by the past you have lived, a role you play, a career you have obtained, or a purpose you fulfill. Those are amazing, necessary, and we are called to some of those, absolutely. When you are able to define yourself in Him, you are learning to remove the focus off yourself, and worldly acceptance, so you can glorify Him with your purpose. Defining yourself in Him does not give you pride; it is not an aged accolade. Instead, these values are timeless gifts built within us that we simply claim from our Creator, and it forever brings Him glory. When you speak of who you are in Him, it glorifies what He has done, not the choice you have made or what you have accomplished, and that is a biography I want others to read. It does not remove the importance of the purpose He has called us to, the roles we fulfill, our special gifts He has granted us, or our achievements. Instead, it allows us to find our true identity as a citizen of the Kingdom of heaven. Redefining our identity in Him is another step in freeing ourselves of the labels we place on ourselves and the worldly view we see in others while glorifying the Creator whose children we truly are.

The day I realized this place is not my home and began accepting the truth of who God says I am, is the day I began walking in the direction of real freedom. We are reminded that this place is temporary, and by this place, I mean our life here on earth. The world itself is not our home; it is only a temporary residence to which we embark in order to fulfill the greatest calling we can possibly achieve—spreading the good news of Jesus, expanding His Kingdom, and growing in Him to be able to fulfill the purpose to which we have been called. "So we fix our eyes not on what is seen, but on what is unseen, since what is seen is temporary, but what is unseen is eternal" (2 Corinthians 4:18). For years I was overshadowed by the opinions of others, living in fear of judgement, trying to progress to a worldly status of achievement. As I grew deeper in my faith with Christ, I started to shed so much of the world. It was a piece of the process so necessary, but I was so completely unaware of it taking place. It wasn't until I fully grasped the concept of who I was in Him, defined by the One who created me, that I finally felt the freedom of following Jesus.

CHAPTER 6

Shedding the World

Father God,

Thank You, Lord God, for creating a world rich in beauty and opportunity to serve you. Father remind me that I am not of this world but only in this world. As Your child, I belong to the Kingdom of Heaven and will face hardships on this earth from those who do not understand my walk with You. Father, grown me in my courage, strength, and perseverance as I press on in faith.

In Jesus' Loving Name I Pray, Amen.

I remember standing at the front of the Sanctuary one Sunday morning as the worship team began to play. This one particular song starts to play, and the lyrics spoke to my current phase of "faith metamorphosis." The rhythm filled the room, and the words spoke to my spirit. The message was simple: *more than anything this world has to offer, Christ is enough.* I am choosing to leave the world behind and follow Jesus Christ. That song became my anthem for that season of growth. It was an amazing reminder of why I didn't need validation from the world, material desires others strived for, or to be concerned with anyone's opinion, trends, or focus. It comforted me when old friends no longer understood me or cared to be around me because I was too weird or a "Jesus freak." As you incrementally transform and redefine your identity, you will slowly begin to shed the world. It is an essential part of maturing in your faith, and one that can come with many growing pains.

During a small group Bible study, a question was posed to our group. I remember this question specifically because I felt mind blown—or faith blown, so to speak. It was also at that moment I realized how "young" I was in my walk compared to those around me. As my mouth dropped open and I gasped this, "whoaaaa" response to the question, others simply smiled in an adoring kind of "aww, isn't she precious."

The question was this, if God did not bless your life in any other way, would Jesus dying on the Cross still be enough? The answer, of course, was yes, but the mind-blowing part was that He still does these amazing, incredible, life-altering things, spiritual gift giving, and transforming things inside of us. Do I genuinely live my daily life with a thankful heart for ALL of these things?

Honestly, salvation should be so much more than enough, and yet, there is so much more that God offers! Christ *is* more than enough for me, but as a newbie on my walk, it was easy to get distracted from all the God-filled awesomeness by the world. I would have to regain focus at Church on Sunday, and then once again at Bible study on Wednesday. My faith-span had some major deficits! What I learned was that this was completely normal, and as I gained knowledge, learned more about Jesus, and figured out those pieces of faith-based discipline, it would help the yo-yoing to be less drastic and my faith walk to be more balanced.

Shedding the world can be full of growing pains, life lessons, uncomfortable conversations and a host of other necessary moves to fulfill growth and freedom in Christ. As we mature in our faith, the things that once fit in our life may not seem to fit so well. Like an old sweater you just can't seem to get rid of, even though it's out of style and hasn't fit for years. The same applies to the friend you have that continues to influence your life in a way that doesn't align with your new-found faith or current season of purpose. Could you imagine marrying the person you dreamt of marrying when you were 13 years old? For some of us, that Tiger Beat centerfold or Jr. High notebook initials just wouldn't make the cut by today's standards and thank God for that!

It is part of our never-ending story where people come into our lives; we grow together, forge lifelong partnerships, or short-term leases, move in, and grow apart. When it comes to love some of us meet our partners in time early on in life, while some of us continue to develop a new ideal every five or so years, re-purposing ourselves and thus the person we envision as our best fit. Logically, yet uncomfortably accepted, this same practice should also be applied to friendships and other personal behaviors.

I truly believe friendships are the underlying goodness of earth; they are these tiny flecks of gold in the very fiber of our beings. For it is our true, genuine friends that observe our most reactionary moments, capturing qualities rivaled by only our parents or our children. They are brought into spaces of ourselves in which we offer only the most sacred of invitations. Some of these friendships withstand the test of time, defying the challenges and struggles of age, distance, physics, and distraction. Then there are those that fall away as individuals change, disconnecting at various crossroads along our way. It is not only a rite of passage, but a vital and fruitful requirement to cut the excess branches away to allow the necessary air and light to get in.

Yet, it seems as we become adults some of these friendships that should have fallen to the wayside, become unnecessary toxic baggage we carry with us. We struggle to shed the world as we grow deeper in our pursuit of faith. Refusing to let go, we will talk ourselves in circles, overridden with guilt, flooding our minds with memories, filling our hearts with fear over potential conflicts, and paralyzing our words so that we are shackled by people who are no longer healthy for our growth.

People who no longer support our path, our faith, or our journey forward, doesn't mean they are bad people. It does mean they no longer compliment or support the environment you could thrive in. Now, I wonder if you are able to see the root of this internal turmoil that wants to keep people bound to unhealthy relationships? You've guessed it, that deceptive thief, prowling around. Toxicity can be especially detrimental for Christians who have rededicated themselves to Christ from a life that was at one time not in line with His Word.

You see, somewhere along the way we started to believe that creating an environment supportive of our faith, by removing elements that distracted us from our walk, was somehow selfish, or unchristian like. We started to believe the lie that if we did this, we were making ourselves better than others by no longer associating with those unbelieving. However, it is quite the opposite. It is imperative to your growth and development as a follower of Christ to remove the impact of people who consistently bring you down, drain your energy, distract you from your faith, your journey, your passion, attending Church, and/or your mission in Christ. The important part here is that while you are growing and working on your faith, there are worldly behaviors and friendships that must be shed in order for you to fully grow and mature.

2 Corinthians 6:14 tells us "do not be yoked together with unbelievers. For what do righteousness and wickedness have in common? Or what fellowship can light have with darkness?" I love the time that I spend with my sisters in Christ, I always leave those conversations refueled, energized, and feeling closer to God. As a single mom, I had very little time to give to friends, but what I realized was that it was time for me to start investing my time with those who I felt invested in my journey, and in my purpose. There were "friendships" that simply existed, because they were just there, and had yet to be audited for what they were in my life now. Time was invested because it was part of a routine, and the conversations, emotions, and results from them were not cultivating a Christ-like mission. So, if I was investing time and conversation into people, topics, and situations that did not help fulfill my mission in Christ, or enrich my spiritual environment for my family, then why was I investing at all?

I want to be clear that when a person comes to faith, it does not mean that they have to cut off every person they associated with that doesn't believe in God or practice faith, quite the contrary. We are to be a light to as many walks of life as possible and spread the Word and love of our Savior. Matthew 5:16 instructs us, "in the same way let your light shine before men, that they may see your good deeds and praise your Father in heaven." What this unevenly yoked means is who we are close to. If we want to grow deeper with Christ, we all need to undergo an impact audit on our faith from time to time. It is pivotal that we take a very close look at the *impact* we allow people to have on our minds, our spirit, our energy. How do they *impact* the time and space we are giving them in our lives, and the energy and support they are providing us on our walk?

A person who offers advice from the world instead of the Word is going to guide you from a very different perspective and support a mission that is not in line with what God has in store for you. Those relationships require close examination, because if we cannot restrict the time, impact, and effect we allow worldly or toxic relationships to have on our growth and development with the Lord, then it is time to remove them in totality from our lives. The enemy will continue to use those relationships to keep you shackled from His purpose. These barriers will be disguised as friendships, relationships, or situation-ships. You may even believe you are working to bring *them* into faith, when at the end of conversations, you are the one left drained and depleted, not lifted and refueled.

There are some very simple questions you can ask yourself to help aid you in auditing your faith. What friends are within your circle an' '~ what degree do they impact your relationship with God? Do they suppc your journey? Do they give you spiritual energy or do they leave you drained? Do they add to the Christ-like environment you are trying to create for your family?

A few years ago, I had to conduct this very same audit on my own life, and it resulted in removing some very close people out of my circle that had been there for years. It was hard and weighed heavy on my heart. The enemy tormented my emotions, filled me with fear of conflict, and had me questioning my character as a Christian. God showed me as I prayed, on more than one occasion, the truth in these relationships, and that those emotions and friendships contradicted the purpose that God had for me. He showed me how our interactions left me with emotions that resulting in anger instead of forgiveness, pettiness instead of empathy, and the world instead of His Word. Not all friendships are forever, and that is okay.

Sometimes we are going to have to make some uncomfortable decisions as adults, especially when it comes to dealing with and impacting other adults' feelings in a way we think might be hurtful or confrontational. In the end, we must remember what *our* purpose is, and who *we* serve. If we involve God in these decisions, working to provide ourselves and our families an environment that is more supportive of a relationship with God, that will never be wrong. Even when those who don't understand that relationship with Him, feel it might be. There may come a time when God is ready for your faith to take flight, but first, you are going to have to check your baggage before you can board.

These are all important steps I had to accomplish before I understood and embraced the freedom offered to those who choose Jesus Christ. Some of it is tough, uncomfortable, even scary. There is this amazing confidence that comes when you put your faith in God, step out in His truth, and walk in His will knowing you are making choices that align with His purpose for your life. Once you give glory to God, once you are open about your broken, once you speak on how He has transformed you, there is nothing in your past that can burden your present. When the people who hold the most impact in your environment support your walk, understand the grace and love of God and help strengthen your stride as you walk out your faith, your empowerment through Christ is limitless.

God knew it all, Jesus took it on the cross, and if my life is for Him, the One and only Judge, then why do I care about the opinions of the world? If my goal is to live with Him in the Kingdom of heaven, then no one here on earth can hold more weight than He does. No one. You answer to God, who has already seen your past, present, and future, and loved you enough knowing it all, to send His only son to die for you on the cross. How could anyone's opinion matter more than God's? If what you say and do brings glory to God, then speak it, live it, and do it all boldly and without fear. That is freedom! Understanding this truth is key to walking boldly in your unique identity and radically living out your faith walk with purpose. You must be surrounded by people who will enrich your walk, who will go into battle with you when needed, and who will speak the Word, not the world, into your life.

Sharing the good news isn't reserved for missionaries who travel to other countries. We are all called as ambassadors of Christ to share the news of who Jesus is and what He is doing in our lives! What better testimony to give than our own; but you can't be shackled in fear of worldly judgment to give it. If you are afraid of what the world is going to say, about what you have to say, you will never say anything at all.

In Mark 16:15 Jesus said to them, "Go into all the world and preach the gospel to all creation." The word gospel is literally an ancient Greek translation that means good news. We are told by Jesus to go and spread the good news with all of the world! Part of your purpose is to share the good news about Jesus. Part of the battle for achieving this is overcoming the fear that many believers face when they simply *think* about talking to others about their faith. Now, add a conversation about what Jesus has done regarding their past spiritual battles, current struggles, or even speaking openly about their love for Jesus, and cue nausea, anxiety, and sweaty palms. People love talking about what their accomplishments. They do not like talking about their weaknesses or failures. God tells us, pride comes before destruction. So lay it down, and give Him the glory.

A Spiritual Battle

Understanding the freedom we are offered in Christ is only a sliver of our journey to living free. There are layers to each Scripture, just as there are layers to each season of your life. How this opportunity of freedom will impact you in your thirties, will be completely different from when you are in your forties, or fifties, and so on. The beauty of this freedom walk is that it is ever-changing. The critical piece is this: just because you're aware of the freedom you are offered, even if you accept it, embrace it, and begin living in it, does not mean you are exempt from the war that will be waged against you to stop you from living in it. This statement is not meant to frighten you. One who walks with Christ should never be afraid of Satan, the enemy flees from Jesus, remember?

We discussed how the enemy attacks, using your past, disguising himself as other things, or guilting you into keeping toxic relationships in your life. We saw how this could be an effective, fiery dart; and how Scripture advises us to defend against the enemy and these attacks. The more you journey on your walk with Christ the more deceptive the enemy will become. His attempts more strategic, tactful, and focused on stopping you from being effective for God. Preparing for the war waged against you is an essential part of your continued growth and maturity in Christ.

Now, I'm not talking about readying for war like cutting carbs and training with dead lifts and cardio exercises. I mean meditating on the Word of God and advancing your prayer life. Honest, thoughtful, prayer specific to the circumstances in your life. Why? Because a Christian who lives freely in Christ is a Christian who is living powerfully for the Kingdom of God. Satan wants nothing more than to bring you down, to distract you with busyness to keep you out of the Word, and to bring you into the chains of the world. He will work to bind you up with stress, worry, fear, and concern of opinions, shame, guilt, and anything else other than the freedom you found in Christ Jesus. I understand some people question the authenticity of the existence of Satan. Some read these statements and roll their eyes, but please know, there are dark forces waging war, every single day. That is very real and failing to acknowledge and prepare your mind and spirit for it, is willful ignorance.

The Apostle Paul said, "the war we are waging is not against flesh and blood, this is a spiritual battle, but just because it cannot be seen does not mean it is not real." Every battle needs preparation and you must be fully aware that as you grow and become more effective in your purpose and ministry, you will need to become more prayerful and defensive with your armor against the enemy. You will need to wage war in the spiritual realm as you progress forward on your spiritual walk. Have the discernment to know the battles you are fighting in life may appear to be life battles but are most likely schemes of the devil to keep you distracted from moving forward on your walk with God.

Even as I was nearing these last chapters of this book, I began thinking of the release. Fear began creeping in as I thought of people that I go to church with reading about how I had an abortion or wondering if someone I worked with would read the past I lived. I cringed at the thought of their judgment. Oh my gosh, what if my kids read it…fear crept in so fast that I started to panic. At that moment I had a choice, to activate my faith and be disciplined in the truth of God or saturate my thoughts in fear. Instantly, I remembered who I lived for, who died for me, and who I will answer to at the end of my days.

When I get to my judgment day, it will not be anyone I go to church with, it will not be anyone that I work with, and it will not be the children I have raised that I will stand before. God knows my story, my steps, and has forgiven me for the sins that I have committed, confessed, and sought genuine forgiveness of. Thankfully, I know that truth and answered the lies the enemy was fueling into my mind with the truth of the Lord. Had I not been prepared for that, I could have found myself swept into shackles of shame like the enemy had used to bind me up years before. It was a spiritual war being waged to stop good works from happening, to stop me from wanting to release this book, to shame me into fear and keep me in bondage. Without knowledge of the truth and who I am in Christ, I could stay in a place of fear, in a place that was not free but enslaved to my past. That same truth applies to you as well. It applies to the hundreds of thousands of millennials who have fallen victim to a spiritual battle that is being waged all around them, right now. People who have been judged by self-righteous people who labeled themselves Christian but were failing to reflect Jesus Christ. People like those damning me to hell, not knowing they were doing the work of the enemy, while holding up signs of Christ the King. We must fight this battle with the truth we know. When you are faced with an opportunity to step out in faith, share your testimony, talk about the incredible works God has done in your life, and be on guard for the enemy to attack.

If God has called you into a new direction in your life that requires you to step out in faith, be ready for the enemy to try and stop you. Acts of faith that are illogical to the world are powerful to the Kingdom and detrimental to the plans the enemy has. If you are prepared for it, then you will know the fear, anxiety, or worry is not real but a scheme to keep you from moving forward. 2 Timothy 1:7 says, "For God hath not given us the spirit of fear; but of power, and of love, and of a sound mind." That is the truth of God you can stand on time and time again.

Freedom in Christ, once understood, should not be considered like that of our freedom in the world. As shown, it will be continually tried, in various ways, and therefore we must be refining our knowledge of the truth. Walking in that freedom will allow us to strengthen the bond to our freedom. If we live in a place of fear or continually welcome fear, our bondage to fear grows, it becomes a comfortable place, easily accessible to us. However, the same then applies to live in the freedom of Jesus Christ. The more we live in the freedom of Christ's truth: knowing to fear not because we are children of God, that through Him all things are possible, that it is He who works all things out for good for those called according to His purpose, and the thousands of other promises and truths that He offers to us, the more our bond to that freedom will be strengthened. It is through that faith-filled discipline that we will build up the freedom to which we can live boldly and confidently.

Living freely in Christ is a journey that must be developed individually. It is specific to each person, as unique as their own creation in Christ, reminded of such perfect individualism for no two fingerprints are the same. He reminds us of His intelligent design, like no other. Unlike freedom in the world, no one else oversees protecting it, building it, or ensuring it's secure on your behalf. The cultivation of that freedom, the assurance of its existence in your life is solely up to you. It is a personal decision, a personal relationship, and a personal development with Christ, that you alone will build and work through.

The amazing part is that no one else is responsible for it! You do not have to depend on anyone else to get this done, you, along with Jesus Christ, can do it. The difficult part is that the enemy's schemes of distraction will seem very appealing to try and prevent you from learning, building, growing, and developing this relationship to allow such a foundation to be developed. These distractions will be just as unique in your life. It is up to you to have the discernment and obedience to press on, to set aside time with God and keep your appointments with Him, no matter how tired you feel that day, or what has come up. You make the time instead of finding the time, and when you make Christ a priority in your life you will start to see the fruits of that obedience and discipline manifest in amazing ways.

CHAPTER 7

The Transparent Christian

Father God,

Thank you for Your faithfulness. Thank You for overseeing Your Word and ensuring that Your promises stand true. I am so grateful to serve a merciful God, whose love for me is reckless and undefined. Father allow these words to resonate in my spirit. Speak to my heart and allow Your will for my life to take root. Help me to walk out the plan that You have for my life, so that I may be bold in my pursuit for You.

In Jesus' Holy and Precious Name, I Pray, Amen.

We are all responsible for our own journey, our own path, our own walk with God. Everyone's walk with Christ begins at a different starting block. We run far different marathons, weather different storms, and will journey through life with varying degrees of brokenness. What if we actually knew the broken that filled the seats of our churches? What if non-believers knew about the transformations that occurred daily within broken people, who chose to let the light in? What if we were more honest about our struggle, our sin, our not so glorious moments when God showed up and changed it all? Would our evangelistic impact be different?

I believe so, and I think it would be in an immeasurable way. Would we still be facing a faith crisis where one in four millennials don't identify with any faith at all? Would more than half of them feel that Christianity is too judgmental? Would Facebook still be filled with people telling others what they are doing wrong, instead of Who loves them more than anything? Would thoughts and prayers be a joke on social media or would it be an authentic response with an understood power?

"I just don't want to be judged," she said, "I'm not like you, I don't have it all together yet. I want to go to church but something might catch fire if I try to walk in." I have heard this statement countless times from people who have a skewed vision of who Christians are, what a genuine church is, and the message that is delivered within those walls. So many people feel this way when it comes to attending church, or finding their faith, especially when they haven't ever been, or have walked away for a while. The idea of Christianity today is painted as a judgmental group of holier-than-thou, religious hypocrites, who stand on Scripture in order to point a finger at others' sin.

So, anxiety creeps in when envisioning some picture-perfect museum of holy togetherness picking apart every piece of their flawed lifestyle, as they choose their seat in the very last row of the sanctuary, hoping to go unnoticed. This idea is so paralyzing that it keeps many from even entertaining the idea of pulling into the church parking lot. Believers who know the truth in Jesus Christ know that the transformation we have discussed occurs *after* you commit to Christ; but how do you deliver that message if you can't get people inside His house to hear it? The call then is for the body of Christ to be boldly authentic in reflecting Jesus and glorifying God's transformation *outside* of the church. The message needs to be seen in living testimony if it can't be heard in Sunday messages. For the authenticity and transparency of our walk to be real, genuine, and honest, we must be bold enough to challenge the flawed perspective the enemy feeds and instead plant and water the truth of Jesus.

The beautiful thing is we are ALL a work in progress. The sad thing is I can identify as the girl who once wanted to wait until I had it all together before I would ever step foot inside a church again. I had walked through sanctuary doors, full of guilt, and a plethora of bad decisions. You can take your pick from the grab bag of what I have shared. At that time, I was a young, single mom, no wedding ring (trust me they checked), wearing jeans, and I am sure I had a spit-up stain, or two, somewhere down the front of my blouse. I know I had heard *come as you are* somewhere before. Apparently there should have been an asterisk beside it. It's not like I had the scarlet letter sewn to my forehead, but the way they were staring, I was clearly out of my element.

Met with a host of disapproving looks and judgmental stares by a congregation basking in self-righteousness, I was more self-conscious than ever. I sat with my son on my lap, just thankful we made it before the sermon began; the last two Sundays were failed attempts. Shortly into the first reading, or maybe the second, as my son was making verbal indications he was not digging the Sunday message, I was met with rolled eyes and a few stare-downs until the gentlemen in front of me turned and huffed as my son started to cry. I fumbled trying to avoid falling over the kneel pad thing and making my way out of the aisle and into the cry room. My face was so red it was on fire, I was mortified.

So much for coming in, or going out, unnoticed. At that time in my life, to say I was exhausted would be a major understatement. I was a full-time grad student, going through a divorce, and trying to manage life as a newly single mom. Life was overwhelming and all I wanted to feel was what I remembered feeling when I went to church with my grandma: comfort, peace, belonging. Yet, judgment was passed based on a storm God allowed me in that those around me knew nothing about. I left before the homily had even ended, tears pouring out of my eyes all the way home. I told myself I was stupid for even attempting to go to church when my life was such a mess. Any time thereafter that I even considered going again, the enemy quickly reminded me of that day.

I stayed angry, but not with God because I felt it was my fault that He disapproved of me being in His house. I was angry at Christians and refused to associate with them, talk about faith, or even consider going to church after that. My sharp turn away from faith started with mass that morning and it took eight years before I stepped foot inside God's house again. Yes, I was church hurt, but that turned into God spite, and it became a continuous eight-year spiral, absent of faith.

Looking back, my faith in Christ should not have been determined by a church or the people who attended it. I can, however, certainly identify with the millennial perspective of a judgmental Christianity as I replay that moment. For many Christians, they fail to understand or acknowledge their responsibility in impacting others perspective of the body of Christ. The church today seems more asleep than ever!

I for one, never had a relationship with Jesus, and that is why when I left the church for good, I left the faith. For me, I had religion. It was all religious order and rules, set motions, or activities that fell within four walls. The self-righteous congregation, that is still as ever-present today mind you, didn't aid in spiritual growth by any means. The church shouldn't solely define, create, or sustain the relationship that you have with Christ. However, it should be a place where you can go and feel the presence of our King and hear His word absent of judgment. It is where you can gather with other believers for fellowship, prayer, and support. At the end of the day, whether you have been there for fifteen seconds or fifteen years, given nothing or given thousands, everyone has equal access and equal belonging in His house, and no one should make you feel different. Jesus Himself says come as you are, and religion has sold too many people something other than that truth.

This is why transparency and openness in our journey with Christ is so important. Not only because it does a great work within us, allowing freedom to be found and experienced, it breaks our chains and catapults our growth. As you see, there is an outward-facing purpose that this transparency and openness serves for the Kingdom that speaks of divine providence. As we share allow ourselves to be vulnerable to glorify God, it breaks down the barriers to allow others inside to experience Him through us. It lets people who are battling their own past see the other side of the transformation, and cites the source, Jesus Himself.

Throughout Scripture God allows us to see how many of His followers are open and transparent about not only their brokenness but also their faithfulness. In Psalms David is beautiful with his transparent struggle and powerful faith. We are shown that it is okay to be vulnerable as a Christian. It is okay to let others know that you sometimes fail. And although we don't know how God is going to use our struggle, we can be certain He will use it for good. I have referenced this Scripture a few times before, but when we face difficulty Paul tells us, as he is writes from prison in Rome, "We know that God causes all things to work together for good to those who are called according to His purpose" (Romans 8:28). We live in a fallen world, and with that comes trials, struggle, hardship, and battles. God promises us that what we go through, if even by our own demise, to those that believe in Him, will be used for good. If Paul can see this by faith, while sitting in prison, writing and encouraging believers, that is certainly something we can hold strong to in our everyday life. I am very open in my walk. Sometimes I mess up, and life still impacts me too in difficult ways. Standing in faith, reflects how I respond. I am a constant work in progress, with emphasis on the word progress. The more open and honest I am about my struggles, my faith, and my journey… the more people are drawn to me with questions and interest about Christ and my journey in building my relationship with Him. People can relate to brokenness because we are all broken, and they can see their own broken within it. Romans 3:23 says, "for ALL have sinned and fall short of the glory of God."

I know God called me to write this book to encourage believers to be open with their transformation, their struggle, and the glory that God has bestowed on their life. Can you imagine a house of God, filled with people, who are genuinely honest about who they are in Christ, but humble enough to know it is *only* through Him that they are transformed? Can you imagine seeing people who walk into Church with the eyes of Jesus and not the eyes of the world? He thought we were all worth dying for, every one of us.

I imagine how different those eight years would have been had I stepped inside those sanctuary doors, to be met with a group of believers who saw my desire to know Jesus, and not the baggage I walked in with. God used that situation for good, as I am now deliberately bold in my faith, overtly transparent in my walk, and able to evangelize to those who are wading in a mess that I remember too clearly. I want people to be comfortable coming to Christ no matter where they are, because those eight years of life I walked absent faith, were some of the hardest years of my life. The crazy part is, I have faced more significant life issues since being saved. Yet, God has walked by my side, keeping me up in His right hand, filling me with unexplainable peace, grace, and an abundance of favor. That is what life is with Christ, and it is our job to help others see that truth! There is no reason to maneuver through life without God!

Don't ever forget that God uses all types of people to fulfill His purpose and expand His Kingdom. As I said before, Jacob was a cheater, Peter had denied Christ, Noah was a drunk, Jonah ran from God, Sara was impatient, David had an affair, Rahab was a prostitute, Joseph was abused, and Lazarus was dead! If you are still breathing, you have a purpose and God is still working on you!

Be open with your broken, because we are all broken, and it is with purpose that God specifically called those broken people to be used. When Jesus Himself came to walk this earth, He did not call into action the Pharisees as many would have thought. He called the people who were the least expected, average, broken people, whose transformation could be seen, and glory given only to God. I know that people will find themselves far more comfortable walking through the doors of the House of the Lord if they knew they were not alone in their struggles. More people would want to know Jesus if the transformation stories included a beginning, not just a person standing proudly at where they are now, failing to acknowledge the process to get there.

The amazing part we learn is that God doesn't transform us just for the sake of ourselves. He matures us in our faith to then put that faith into action to be used for His Kingdom; to be called out onto the water. God says, "I will use it for good for those who are called according to My purpose" (Romans 8:28). Once you invite God in and allow Him to start working in your life, all of that mess becomes part of your testimony. The past becomes experiences to use in ministering to other people who may be going through that same mess. People who have yet to allow God into their situation or even their life. When your perspective shifts and you are able to see how God can use the past to minister to others in your present, your entire outlook on struggle changes. You can truly count it all as joy because you know there is a greater good in all of it.

Two years ago, I was diagnosed with multiple sclerosis. As I've said, I am a single mom of two very active kids, ages thirteen and nine. I work a full-time career and live an active lifestyle that includes sports, travel, community events, volunteering; our family is always on the move. I am the third in my immediate family to be diagnosed with this disease, and my form had been determined to be aggressive. In my first year I faced seven relapses, all of which were attacks on my optic nerves, each ended with a five-day steroid treatment at the hospital's infusion center.

It was from this diagnosis that I decided I would start writing again. I wanted to battle the disease with faith. I wanted to write articles about my journey of growing closer to Christ any time I felt myself being overwhelmed with sadness or fear. I didn't know how this disease was going to progress, but I was making the choice to praise God through it all in advance. I was preparing to be disciplined in faith because I knew there would be opportunities for the enemy to attack in various stages of vulnerability.

The first article I wrote, God called me to submit it for publishing. God called you? Not on my cell phone, but yes. The more you grow in faith the more you know when God is moving you to act, to pursue, to move. It was not part of my plan to publish these, in fact, I had never considered such a thing, and had to *google* to even know where to begin. Thus, after a few hours of googling later, I submitted for publishing. That article was not only accepted but published three days later. In just a matter of hours, it was shared over ten thousand times!

I was in awe of how God took a piece of my broken and used it to bless others on their journey. I received messages from women as far away as Kenya, thanking me for my honesty and transparency. I prayed with a woman in Nicaragua over a situation she was struggling with. I remember sitting at my laptop one evening, just in utter amazement of how God took my transformation story, and my battle response, and used it to affect so many people. Months later that same article had reached hundreds of thousands of people across the world. Little old me, publishing my very first article, trying to deal with a diagnosis, while God worked it all out for good. He honors our discipline and blesses others in the process.

As I continued to be more open with my struggles and operate in unwavering faith, the response from others was astounding. I was clinging to God, growing tremendously in my faith, and others were witness to my love for Him despite the chaos in the world around me. Some were shocked, others thought it was a crutch, but two and a half years later, many more have asked me about Jesus than I could have ever fathomed. Faith in action proves to be a powerful testimony, especially when they know your broken past. When God takes broken, restores, redeems, and then brings an unexplainable peace amongst a present, raging hurricane… that is something outsiders look at and desire.

The more I became aware of how my transparency could expand the Kingdom of God, the more I began looking for opportunities in every situation I was in. God put people in my path that needed to hear my mess because most of the time, it was just like their own. God waited until I was aware of the need for boldness, until I removed the power of the enemy over my past and truly accepted God's grace, before He called me to this new-found purpose. An untested vessel won't be put to sea.

My Grandpa used to say when you want advice on your finances, don't ask the basket weaver. The same can be applied to faith. It is easier to listen to someone who has had experience walking through the fire and coming out on the other side, than someone who is talking about something they never lived through or only read about. There are many times a person's introduction to Jesus comes from observing those that follow Him. Dwight Lyman Moody said it best, "of 100 unsaved men, 1 will read the Bible, 99 will read the Christian." If we are open with sharing our testimony, our walk with God through the trials, then the effectiveness of our personal ministry is limitless. God will use you in ways you would have never imagined and in situations that you didn't expect. We have to see faith in our own experiences to understand how pivotal it can be in expanding His Kingdom or deepening the faith of fellow believers.

I remember one day as I sat in the parking lot, thinking of the last time I was in that infusion center following another relapse from my MS. I smiled thinking of the woman I had met that was undergoing chemotherapy. She was fighting her second battle. Her hair was gone, and she wore her bald proudly, beautifully. Her personality was spunky, and we talked and laughed so much it made an hour seem like ten minutes.

They say first impressions are the greatest; well hers changed my entire life. She had walked past me pulling her IV cart and she paused, her smile faded, and she said, "oh no, no, no, you are far too young and far too pretty to be in here, and they put you in the back, huh?" I just laughed and said, "oh yeah, well I'm a repeat offender, so they keep us troublemakers back here I guess." She asked what I was fighting, and I let her know it was Multiple Sclerosis. She told me how she was going to beat her cancer, and then go travel the world, and I told her that was exactly what we were going to claim. She then took my hand, leaned in close, and looked me in the eye. It was in that moment that I knew she was about to share something with me about this fight that only someone who knew these battles could. She said, "It may seem a lot different, but it's not. We are both fighting for our lives; me, to keep mine, but only for a set amount of time, and you, for the quality and duration of yours, but for the entirety of it. Do not lose your smile. Do not lose your faith. Do not stop laughing, no matter what. Just love more, love harder, laugh louder, and grow wiser. Spend all your time with the people you love or doing things that you love. And when you can, travel, see it all."

She gave my hand a squeeze, popped up, and said *yep*, we will be just fine. Will I see you tomorrow, same time? And with tears welling up in my eyes, I simply said *yep*.

She blessed me so much in that place, in an unexpected moment; God sent me an angel. I was seriously struggling during that infusion. She had no idea, but it was my fourth and I had begun treatment that was far more painful than I had anticipated. To be honest I was worn out and beyond discouraged. Yet, right then she changed my entire perspective and I realized I too could be a light in a place of darkness. It took a woman who was fighting a battle far harder than my own to make me realize that. I could use these opportunities to uplift others in their battles, or I could wallow in my own pity. I could continue to walk in flesh, serving no purpose to the Kingdom, bringing no glory to God, or I could choose to be the disciple He calls me to be. How could I call myself a child of God yet not reflect it in a place His light was needed the most? It was there my battle perspective changed. With an IV pumping in my arm, with tears streaming down my face, with an angel sent from God just a few chairs away, I traded flesh for faith.

Our entire world can change in a single moment. Maybe it is a significant loss, losing your career, financial devastation, or an array of other life-altering stresses. Life as we know it changes, but how we respond to that change, literally determines the impact that situation has on us, and everyone around us. This new-found struggle can become a blessing if you allow it to be. It is an opportunity to grow His Kingdom and insurmountably in your faith; remembering that *perspective* is everything, and *choice* is key. "When you pass through the waters, I will be with you; and through the rivers, they shall not overwhelm you, and when you walk through fire, you shall not be burned, and the flame shall not consume you" (Isaiah 43:2).

To utilize this storm in a way that contradicts everything that our flesh wants us to do, we are therefore acting on faith and faith alone. Fear not, know that I am God and I am with you, praise Me and share the message of My love and My works. Our flesh wants us to be tired, disappointed, discouraged, and side effected. The enemy sees our vulnerability and wants us to doubt the goodness of God and the strength of who He is. And don't get me wrong there will be moments that those things occur and all we can control are the thoughts that run through our mind as we battle through the pain, exhaustion, tears, while literally crawling to the bed, praying to God, and the power comes when we still say the words, *thank you, Father*. In those moments, despite our flesh, we are firm in faith.

Before I walked into the infusion center, I smiled, thanked God for giving me this opportunity, and prayed for Him to use me. Allow me, Lord, to be a light in the darkness. Allow me to uplift those around me, to overcome the sadness that may fall as I look around at the struggle. Let me fill others with love, strength, and laughter. I choose faith. I choose You. I got out of my car, walked through the center doors, and was greeted by the most amazing nurses I have ever had the pleasure of being cared by. We made a few jokes about how I must have really missed them to be back so soon, and I took a seat in a middle aisle. It wasn't but ten minutes later I was in conversation with the women around me, laughing, joking about our children, and the stresses of raising teens, giving and receiving advice and lessons learned. We laughed with the nurses, and the center no longer felt of a sterile group of strangers fighting these day in and day out battles. Even if just for an hour, it was light; it was faith.

God can use your past or present to change someone else's outlook on life in an instant. We must prepare to be bold, to be transparent, to be open with our broken, and acknowledge Who is responsible in seeing us through. God doesn't call you to pretend, to wear a mask, or to spray on religion when you are in front of others and call it faith. He calls us to be real, to be who He created us to be, and to reflect His son, Jesus Christ.

I wrote before about the Gospel of Mark 16:15, when Jesus said, "Go into all the world and preach the Good News to everyone." The Good News is the salvation and grace given to those who choose to follow Jesus Christ.

It is one thing to say, Jesus is really awesome, you should follow Him, it will change your life. It is another to say, this is who I was, this is the weight that I carried, and this is how my life has changed since I gave my life to Jesus Christ. The first is as if you are talking about a movie you watched or a book you read, simply giving your review. The latter is an explanation of an experience. A direct cause and effect with all reason for transformation given to Jesus Christ. Think of your own decision-making process. You are more apt to choose a restaurant, a mechanic, or a physician, based on an experience someone else had and they shared with you. The same goes for sharing the Good News of Jesus Christ. Your personal experience is everything, and the more open you are about what He has done in your life, the more opportunity you have for others to see His transformative works. If they can see a part of themselves in your story, and you are standing before them renewed, you are living hope before them. That is the powerful, living testimony of Jesus Christ.

"In all this you greatly rejoice, though now for a little while you may have had to suffer grief in all kinds of trials. These have come so that the proven genuineness of your faith—of greater worth than gold, which perishes even though refined by fire—may result in praise, glory and honor when Jesus Christ is revealed" (1 Peter 1:6-7). God is telling us that a faith that perseveres through the fire, that while we go through trials we choose to rejoice in the Lord, brings glory and honor on judgment day. If we can share that story with others, just know there is much glory that we are bringing to God. "Therefore, we do not lose heart. Though outwardly we are wasting away, yet inwardly we are being renewed day by day. For our light and momentary troubles are achieving for us an eternal glory that far outweighs them all" (2 Corinthians 4:16-17).

CHAPTER 8

That's How the Light Gets In

Father God,

Thank You for working every circumstance, every struggle, every trial out for good. Thank You for knowing what is best for me far better than I could ever know for myself. Help me trust you, and find joy in my trials, knowing that there is a refining of my faith and a message to be gained through every one allowed. You will never give me more than I can bear. You are such an amazing Father, and I am so incredibly blessed to be loved by You.

In Jesus' Name I Pray, Amen.

I was scrolling through Pinterest searching for a recipe that I would save and possibly, one day, think about making but more than likely not, when I came across the most beautiful Ernest Hemmingway quote. Have you ever read something that struck you down to your core? You feel what the author or songwriter is saying on multiple levels. I was preparing the content for the first chapter of this book and when I read it, I knew that this would somehow be intertwined into this path God was leading me on. "We are all a little broken, that's how the light gets in" Ernest Hemmingway.

Hemmingway is most widely known as one of the greatest writers of the 20th century and a Nobel prize winner. However, what many don't know is that he was also born a Protestant and converted over to Catholicism as an adult. It is no surprise to me that someone who struggled with brokenness, as Hemmingway did his entire life, would understand this deep faith-based statement in the way that I did. We are all broken, sin-filled, unworthy of Jesus, yet because of this, that is how He gets in.

I want you to picture a crack in a cave wall, it is dark all around, but at the very tip top part of the cave marks a crack. When the sun passes over, the light shines through illuminating the area inside. For us, this is indicative to the way a "crack" in your life that cannot be fixed, healed, or repaired by our own efforts, allows for God's light into our life. Illumination serves as transformation by the Holy Spirit, and the redemption begins.

By the time I finally allowed God to begin working I didn't have cracks, no I was broken in pieces and scattered across the floor. I needed super glue, staples, a hammer, some nails, and any other type of adhesive possible to put me back together. In fact, God probably would have had an easier time just melting me down and starting over with the mold, ya know what I mean? In actuality, that complete breaking was exactly what I needed. Seven years of walking with God and working on myself has been the most incredible process. The only relationship I have been in, is with Jesus. He did not, however, put me back together. No, in fact, I am a completely, utterly, amazing, new creation in Christ.

The person I was, knew nothing of living for Christ, so she lacked real purpose. She didn't know her worth in Christ, so she lacked true self-confidence and security. She certainly didn't live as a reflection of Jesus, so she failed to move in love and inner peace. His light transformed me from the inside out, but it was during that place of absolute brokenness, and utter despair that allowed me to finally turn to the light and allow Him in. If I wasn't broken, if I hadn't felt like a bomb had been detonated inside myself had I not realized that I desperately needed to be rescued, would I have ever sought God to move in my life?

I understand not everyone goes through those times of desperation, but for me, it was necessary. God continues to renew my mind, which renews my thoughts, my actions, and allows me to journey a completely different and impactful life. I continue to grow closer to Him, using many of those scars and battle wounds to minister to other people with scars and battle wounds similar to mine, they just haven't let the light in yet.

When I first was diagnosed with Multiple Sclerosis I struggled a bit with understanding how God was going to use this for good, how this was going to be part of His plan? There were times when I really struggled with putting into action "giving God thanks in all circumstances." Especially when I was going through spinal taps, infusions, and painful injections. I wasn't ever thankful for those specific moments, but I gave Him thanks for the neurologists and modern medicine that I had access too.

See, I know I serve a good God. I know that God is a God above all things, but I also know I live in a fallen world. One full of sin, sickness, and things that God did not create, but that have manifested. God does not force us to love Him, He does not force us to do anything, as humans were given free will.

We should therefore always stand on the promise that when things happen to us, God will work it out for good for those who are called according to His purpose, to those who have chosen God with their free will. In James 1:2-4, I have lived this Scripture as it came alive in my own faith walk. Before I was diagnosed with MS my faith was growing but I was not actively living it. I was pursuing God, attending Bible study, worshiping at Praise and Worship Night, but it's as if I was attending but not in His presence, if that makes sense. I was there but my spirit wasn't activated or fully engaged. The light bulb was screwed in and even turned on, but the dimmer switch was set on low.

I was still a few years into my walk after being saved, so I had nothing to compare it to, occasionally, I would get goose bumps and that was cool, and here and there I would have inspiring conversations or wow moments. I thought I was doing exactly what I was supposed to be doing.

My diagnosis process wasn't exactly normal and I think I should share this to help enlighten you on how this Scripture came to life for me. I was driving home at night from my parent's, which is about a two-hour drive on the interstate, and noticed the lights coming at me seemed double. When I closed my left eye everything seemed normal, when I closed my right eye it was as if I didn't have my glasses on, only I did. My vision without my glasses on is about 20/120 so I can't see very well at all without lenses. I closed each eye back and forth several times looking at different road signs until I was certain there was a significant difference between my eyes. That's when I started to panic and I called my mom.

To be honest, the first thing I thought was MS. This may seem random to others, except that my uncle has MS, my mother has MS, and if you go one step out in my extended family there are another four cousins and two aunts that had been diagnosed with it as well. So, I am no stranger to this disease and the loss of eye-sight in one eye is exactly the first symptom my mom had when she was diagnosed twelve years ago. I called her as I was driving, hands-free of course, and asked her what it was like when she had lost her vision. I told her what was going on and I know she could sense the panic in my voice. She assured me I had been traveling a lot the past couple of weekends, had a stressful few days and she was sure it was stress related. I needed to just get home and get some sleep and it would be fine in the morning. I could sense the worry-filled reassurance in her voice.

When I woke up the next day my vision was even worse. When I moved my eye, I felt pain and as weird as it sounds I could actually feel my eye inside the socket. I felt the urgency in my core, so I contacted an eye doctor who was open on Sunday and told them what was happening. They told me to come there immediately. That's never something you want to hear from a doctor. They did some sort of scan on my optic nerve and could see swelling on the nerve, so they sent me straight to the emergency room. Before sending me, the eye doctor told me I was facing three very serious options: optic neuritis which is correlated with MS, a tumor on the other side of my optic nerve causing pressure and swelling, or I had a brain bleed.

She said they needed to do an MRI and determine the cause immediately. I was given the printouts to take with me and headed straight to the ER. As I was driving myself to the hospital, I remember thinking it was kind of crappy that Multiple Sclerosis was my best-case scenario.

I sat in the ER for nearly eight hours, wondering how much blood one could collect in the brain if it was in fact bleeding. Finally, at around midnight a resident neurologist came in and let me know I had optic neuritis, and they saw lesions on my brain consistent with MS. However, apparently, an ER diagnosis doesn't stick for insurance. Thus, I started my health insurance nightmare of seeing five doctors, over the next five months, endless blood work, a spinal tap, and other various exams. I suffered three more attacks on my eyes while awaiting treatment, each resulting in a five-day steroid infusion before I finally got an insurance approved diagnosis and could start injection treatment. The diagnosis was still in fact, multiple sclerosis. Shocking, I know. This entire process became a new broken. Yes, we can become broken even after we have found Christ. We aren't ever exempt, I wish there was some sort of protection clause, but that's just not how it works.

The injections were three times a week and it turned out I was allergic to the solution it was mixed with, so it felt like acid once it injected into my body. It hurt so bad I would cry and ball up into the fetal position for about thirty minutes. It was excruciating. The neurologist asked me to give it 6 months before they would switch me to a new kind. Insurance likes to see six months of trying before they consider it an actual failure, and level death burning isn't an actual allergic reaction like hives or a breathing reaction. It was six months of cruel and unusual self-torture and I had another four attacks on my eyes during that time. I did grow very close to the nursing staff at the Memorial Infusion Center. I cannot stress enough, how beyond amazing that staff is.

By May the neurologist told me to prepare for blindness. I am not sure that is something any person can legitimately prepare for, but a single mom in her thirties trying to raise two young children, there's not an app for that. I couldn't even grasp the concept, so instead, I clung to God. My neuro didn't know why my MS was so aggressive or why it was just attacking my optic nerves, but they were already seeing atrophy on my optic nerves. Atrophy is when part of the nerve basically dies and there is nothing you can do to get it back. When a part of a nerve dies the signal sent through that nerve is permanently interrupted. I had lost a few small pieces of my vision in my field vision test but nothing major from the first three attacks.

I was clinging to God throughout this entire process in a way that I had never clung to Him. Through every infusion, through every appointment. I would pray through every injection because they were so painful. I had people at church constantly praying for me, putting oil on me, I was writing more articles and they were reaching hundreds of thousands of people. I was serving God, worshipping without boundaries, feeling His presence with me in the darkest hours. My faith grew in a way that I didn't know was possible; I was a living, breathing testimony. The light was illuminating through this broken in a way that was necessary for me to have the strength and perseverance to get through it day after day.

A year later, I had switched my injections to one that doesn't burn. I never went blind and the attacks on my eyes stopped. Last May I went and had my vision checked and after seven attacks in my first year, with documented atrophy on my optic nerves, my vision has actually improved! The optometrist had to check my results three times, to be sure his reading was accurate. I was up to running two miles a day and I participate in CrossFit and HIIT training. I am in the best shape I have ever been in my entire life. I manage MyFaithLift on Facebook which is an offset from the blog I started that now has over 26,000 followers and provides faith-based inspiration. Dana Goodrum Ministry now offers an online store, features other writers, has warfare and protection prayers, and will be one of the main sources for the publicity of this very book!

James 1:2-4 says, "Consider it pure joy, my brothers and sisters whenever you face trials of many kinds, because you know that the testing of your faith produces perseverance. Let perseverance finish its work so that you may be mature and complete, not lacking anything." I stand today thankful for my disease, because without it, I would not have become truly dependent on Christ. I would not have persevered and matured in my faith in such a way that allowed me to surrender control, surrender my day, surrender my life to Him. There were nights when side effects from the injections *and* the infusions combined, and I felt the worst pain I ever had. I would lay in bed and cry so quietly because I wouldn't want my kids to hear. I didn't want them to ever worry or be afraid because it was just the three of us.

I prayed fervently and desperately to God. It was just Him and I in those conversations, and God was the only one who knew my pain, who knew my fears, who knew the depths of where my mind went. God walked with me, day after day, He got me through. Some days He would whisper gentle reminders of His promises, of Scripture that I would turn to in the Bible and it would reaffirm that He was with me, strengthening my faith in magnificent ways. He walked with me every single moment, every dark hour. Jesus was with me in a present form that I cannot ever truly explain. My disease allowed my faith to become anchored.

My faith is unwavering but earned through trial. God walked with me through those trials, and I would gladly go through all of them again because I know without them I would not be where I am in my faith. Yes, knowing the pain that I went through, I would gladly accept it all again, because my faith would not be where it is today without it. That is how much I grew because of those struggles. That is how that Scripture from James came to life on my journey. I see what Paul was trying to say. If in the trials you cling to God, He will use it for good, He will grow your faith, and you will look back and truly count it as joy. You will be able to say, I would go through that again because of how much I matured in my faith. I would choose Multiple Sclerosis every time, because of the intimacy and unwavering faith I now have with Jesus Christ.

I am thankful for those trials that brought me to the depths of my faith but let me be clear, they are not required to be transformed, renewed, and firm in your foundation with Jesus. That was just *my* walk. It was what I needed to become bold enough, free enough, and unaffected by the fear of what the world might think to put all my broken into a book knowing that I would be judged by those around me, knowing others would find strength and hope in my transformation story.

As I wrote earlier, God doesn't call the qualified He qualifies the called, and there is a second vital part to that Scripture that I didn't share in Chapter 4. 2 Corinthians 12:9, "But he said to me, 'My grace is sufficient for you, for my power is made perfect in weakness.' Therefore, I will boast all the more gladly about my weaknesses, so that Christ's power may rest on me." *My power is made perfect in weakness*, what incredible words from Jesus to each and every one of us. He recognizes that we are broken, full of weakness, but through Jesus Christ, we are made whole, through His transformation, we are made new.

If we can cling to Him in our trials, if we can boast about our transformation, including the broken places in which we started, even more glory will be given to God's power and mercy. How powerful will your testimony be if you can talk about your past, your present weakness, with all focus giving glory to God? To know that only through Him are you who you are now, a work in progress, whose weakness is constantly fulfilled by God's grace. Your own message becomes a constant reminder of our humility and His mercy.

I've referenced several times about the current faith-crisis we are facing. Research shows the millennial generation is less involved in faith than any prior generation. Dr. Alex McFarland writes in his article, "Ten Reasons Millennials are Backing Away from God and Christianity,"

> *According to Pew Research Center millennials are the least outwardly religious American generation, where 'one in four are unaffiliated with any religion, far more than the share of older adults when they were ages eighteen to twenty-nine.*

Just over sixty percent of millennials say that Christianity is judgmental.'

The term judgmental is defined as "having or displaying a critical point of view" regarding another's behavior or choices. From my own experiences I previously shared, I can completely understand why this perception exists among this generation. We whisper about the struggle, keep quiet about the strongholds, request prayer as if it is a sign of weakness, when Paul himself tells us to boast for in that weakness is where God can be glorified! Why do we think we have a story absent of God's amazing grace? We are unable. We are not enough. We are ill-equipped. With Christ, we can do all things, achieve all things, conquer all things. We must understand that in our flesh, however, we are nothing but a vessel.

Freedom in Christ means not caring about judgment from the world or being judged by the person sitting next to you in the pew on Sunday. Your walk is between you and God because it will be Him you face in the end. I want to be able to look at Him and say, "Father, I told everyone about the mess I was in and what you delivered me from. I shared the Good News! I never once pretended to be perfect but only through You was I able to be anyone worthy of serving Your Kingdom." What good is a testimony if you keep it to yourself? What good is a movie if you only see the ending?

Jesus tells us to share the good news about Him and He tells us WE are the light and we are to share the good *in us* with others to glorify our Father in heaven! Matthew 5:14-16 says, "You are the light of the world. A town built on a hill cannot be hidden. Neither do people light a lamp and put it under a bowl. Instead, they put it on its stand, and it gives light to everyone in the house. In the same way, let your light shine before others, that they may see your good deeds and glorify your Father in heaven." Jesus is telling us to share our light, our good news about what He has done in our lives because He is love, hope, and truth. Sharing this news with others will always glorify our Father in heaven!

My testimony wouldn't hold near as much weight if you didn't know the mess I had walked through. If I wrote this as a Christian woman, who attends Church on Sunday, serves in youth ministry, leads junior high youth group and women's Bible study, and writes Christian articles for various publications, but removed all of the struggle, lessons, and mess from these chapters, you would be left with a whole lot of religion absent any relationship. The development of my relationship with Jesus, the depth of my transformation, comes when I share the rescue, the burdens, the battle, His mercy and my love for Him. The real opportunity to glorify our Father in heaven would be lost without understanding the depth of the transformation.

Yes, I am writing this as a Christian woman who serves in those capacities, but because those works don't validate who Christ is in me. Prideful biography, remember? Those actions of service serve the Kingdom, but they don't glorify God in the same manner. The real glory comes when you can see how He took me from broken to renewed, how He took my fears and turned them to strengths, how He took my shame and left me with His grace. Only God can do something so extraordinary.

Without the mess, you would miss the message, and God would fall short of really getting the glory that He so deserves in this ever-developing story. So be open with your broken—the past broken, the current broken. Be honest, ask for prayer, talk to your faith circle, and be open with God. When you talk about your transformation, start from the beginning, your own chapter one. Allow yourself to begin reaching out to those who feel they are unreachable because they never knew your broken, and they didn't know that being broken was an opportunity for the light to get in and God to do some of His greatest work. If we don't talk about it, if as believers, we aren't open, honest, and transparent about our mess, people will miss out on the real message and we will fall short on being the genuine body of Christ we are called to be amidst an ever-growing crisis of faith.

As Hemmingway says, we are all a little bit broken, that's how the light gets in...

Tears down her face, hands to the air, in a one-bedroom apartment.
With more ends than means, two kids to feed, she was drowning in the darkness.
And if there was a letter on her chest those at church would've sworn it was scarlet.
She turned her back that day, and never went back, guess you can't have God unless you're on the right track.
She thought of that now.
Will He even hear me as I'm crying out loud?
I've been hiding from Him for so long now...
And just as she opened her mouth to pray, Satan steps in and fills her mind with shame.
Remember all the mistakes you've made?
You think someone like you deserves to be saved?
Her hands drop down and she covers her face...
Then to Satan's surprise she screams out in pain... "Lord help me please, there's not much more I can take.
I can't do this alone; I've made so many mistakes.
I feel like I'm drowning, I just want to be saved..."

Fast-forward to salvation through His amazing grace...

It begins with a reintroduction: I am redeemed.
One prayer saved me from my own never ending bad dream.
For years enslaved believing I was unworthy.

Shackled by self-righteous guilt empowered by the clergy.

*Just hoping one day I could get it together. Make it back to church,
find God, and life would be better.*

But the truth is the message I never knew until later.

The One that broke my chains, restored my soul, and gave me favor.

No one is worthy, that was the whole deal.

Hence, the sacrifice for ALL of us on Redemption Hill.

See, Jesus saw ALL of our sin, ALL of our mess, and our mistakes.

He chose US anyway, and fills us with grace.

*And if you doubt what I say, His Word says this: "My grace is
enough for you, My power is made perfect in your weakness."*

This means He doesn't call the qualified, He qualifies the called.

You don't have to get it together before you talk to God.

He turns mess into messages, it's kind of His thing.

So just come as you are, you don't need a thing.

*Had I known then what I know now, I would've called out sooner
to the One who is crowned.*

For more information or
to schedule a speaking engagement, go to:
danagoodrum.com

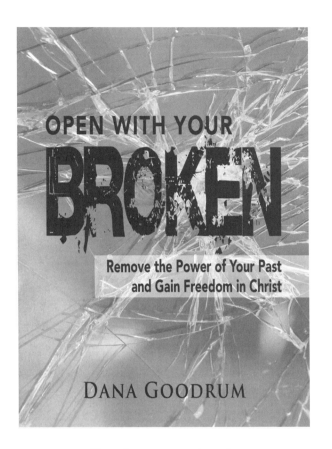

To order more copies of

OPEN WITH YOUR

Order online at:
• www.CertaPublishing/OpenWithYourBroken
• or call 1-855-77-CERTA

Also available on Amazon.com

Certa
PUBLISHING